GHOST ENCOUNTERS
ROYALS & ROGUES

The ghost hunter case files
MARGO WILLIAMS

Edited and produced by Nick Hammond

TEMPLE WAY PUBLISHING

Produced by Nick Hammond
for Temple Way Publishing
Caxton House
Old Station Road
Ventnor
Isle of Wight
PO38 1DX

Printed in the Isle of Wight.
Crossprint Ltd.
Newport Business Park
Barry Way
Newport. PO30 5GY

GHOST ENCOUNTERS
ROYALS & ROGUES

ISBN 978-0-9576051-5-2

CONTENTS

FOREWORD

For over 30 years Isle of Wight-based psychic Margo Williams discovered the best-documented evidence to confirm the existence of ghosts. Her work has been tested and independently confirmed, even by scientists and observed by film teams, all of whom have been amazed by the experience, for Margo Williams recorded the spoken testimony of ghosts and recovered artefacts lost, hidden or buried by the person when still alive.

Most of these case files are from the Isle of Wight, for there are rogues aplenty to be found haunting its buildings and roaming its spooky open spaces. But ghostly royals are more difficult to find, and so this selection also features some of the UK's most famous haunted palaces and castles: Tower of London, the Queen's House, Greenwich, and Windsor Castle.

It is extraordinary evidence, and even more so to be present as many have been to witness this activity. The research confirms the witness accounts of those who have had near-death experiences, and so advances the case for the continuation of personality after the death of the body; but some it seems do not make it through the famous 'tunnel of light' and their physical bodies are in no condition to be reanimated. They are stuck between worlds, earthbound: ghosts. And what they have to say about the experience is most interesting.

So, let them tell you how it is.

CHAPTER ONE

CARISBROOKE CASTLE
THE GHOST OF THE BATTLEMENTS

A GHOST is often seen roaming the battlements of Carisbrooke Castle, and some people believe it to be the sad lost soul of doomed King Charles I who was imprisoned here in the mid 1600s. But those who have seen the ghost up close say it seems to be from an earlier period than the 17th century.

For many years people have tried to identify the ghost of the battlements, and to which period of this castle's long history it belongs. Some say it is one of the great Norman lords, the de Redvers family, who built this castle and from which they ruled the island until the last daughter, Isabella de Fortibus on her death-bed, signed away possession to King Edward I, 'Longshanks'. Others say it is the ghost of sharp-eyed marksman Peter de Heyno, tirelessly manning the ramparts with his bow; the archer whose good aim resulted in the death of the commander of a French invasion fleet.

I first saw the ghost of the battlements as a lone misty figure high up above where I stood near the castle gate. I sensed that he wanted me to climb

Carisbrooke Castle, Newport, Isle of Wight

the inner steps up to the top, but I am glad I did not, for there was something distinctly unsettling about his presence. Perhaps the long years of haunting had turned his mind. Or perhaps he was disturbed of mind long before he ever became a ghost of Carisbrooke Castle.

I saw him on the west wall near the old arrow loop that bears de Heyno's name; and it may be that the ghost dates to this period, although he did not confirm he was there, alive, in the year 1377 when the French force came to Carisbrooke. The French landed at Yarmouth and set fire to the town, then advanced eastward, destroying Newtown on their way inland. Constable of the castle, Sir Hugh Tyrell, watched from the battlements as the force made camp at safe shouting distance from the castle gate; a mass of flags, swords, tents and fires. There were too many to go out and fight, so Sir Hugh and his men checked their provisions, planned for a siege situation and waved two fingers at the enemy; so every Frenchman knew what that meant - damned English archers.

For days thereafter the enemy wandered around the walls staring up and taunting Sir Hugh to stop hiding; and sneering all sorts of other unpleasant innuendo. Days passed and the French took to amusing themselves as best they could; and unfortunately fell into daily habits, including the commander who after breakfast each morning, and supper each evening came close to taunt the defenders with his estimation of English valour and of how Crecy and Poitiers were lucky outcomes won by the bastard sons of lousy English whores. And each morning and each evening the same chorused gesture greeted him from the battlements.

And so the French and English fell into uncomfortable custom; until one evening the commander, through boredom, dined more fulsomely than was wise, and bent to relieve himself several metres closer to the west wall than was safe. And so from his loophole, keen-eyed archer Peter de Heyno struck lucky.

The French camp upped-sticks and backed well beyond dangerous range and then sent word to Sir Hugh they would not go away unless they were paid 1000 marks for the death of their leader. Sir William de Montacute, who commanded the defence of the south coast, was informed and agreed to their demand, though it was the islanders who paid for it in extra taxes; and also helped pay for a makeover for the old Gothic castle when it was given to Sir William as his reward.

That celebrated loophole is still to be found in the castle walls, and was of particular fond remembrance when some ten years or so later, Sir William himself came to Carisbrooke, appointed Lord of the Isle of Wight. Given the castle 'free of rent', he ordered the constable's quarters removed and built

The haunted battlements, looking towards Heyno's arrow loop, Carisbrooke Castle

within these walls a residence fit for a king; and so it proved to be.

In no way do I presume the ghost of the battlements was the ghost of Sir William de Montacute, whose family's bravery in the service of the crown earned great reward and commendation. Doubtless during this castle's long history many strong men named William walked its battlements, feasted in its hall and cruelly abused household servants. Murdering Englishmen was not exclusively a French pastime. Nor were Frenchmen the only target for the English. Sometimes it was just a matter of being in the wrong place at the wrong time, with the wrong information; regardless of whose side you were supposed to be on; as the ghost of the battlements explained to me:

"... I, William, tried to draw thee up upon the walls where many walk, yet thinkest of nothing but their pleasure," he growled. "Why wouldst thee not climb those steps? Yet it seemest thou can free me from mine eternal roaming round and round these walls. A ghostly figure of what was once a strong man who also thought of pleasure - the pleasure of killing a servant who displeaseth me, and knew too much of how I cheated those who put their trust in me. Servant he may be, but he had friends who would taketh their revenge.

A dark moonless night. He leaned over the wall. I followed silently, a quick push and his life was over. I was safe, no one to betray me. A sad accident 'twas said.

I then liveth a happy life with ne'er a thought for this cruel deed. Yet this sin was not forgotten. I did not reach the light that awaits us at our death. I was back where this perfidious task took place. Have had to bide my time, yet can now confess and travel on to heaven or hell. But thanks be, away from the castle walls."

Without a surname we can only wonder over his identity, for he gave no indication of whether he was a resident or a guest. But by his language I think he predated the most infamous period in Carisbrooke's history, when the castle became notorious not for whom it kept out, but the king it kept in.

*   *   *

Although psychic from childhood, I was unaware of any talent for hearing ghosts until my middle years, and when it happened it was quite a surprise for my scientist husband Walter and me. Initially I did not go into haunted buildings to find ghosts; they came to me in my own home. Indeed this is how my work started, as I have related in the accompanying book *Heaven &*

Hell. Briefly to recap: while I was working in the kitchen, a woman spoke to me and then over several days told me in verse the story of her life, of how she had lived in a Devon country town near the sea, and died at an early age. She was the first but not the last. In fact when one had finished another came to speak. When I told my husband of these incidents he was sceptical; an analytical chemist he reasoned that this was some strange side-effect of the menopause through which I was passing and it would disappear. But these people who came to talk to me were telling me all sorts of things about themselves, names and dates, and details of their lives; so Walter decided to prove that they were hallucination by writing to historians and newspapers and archive departments in the towns where these people claimed to have lived and died.

But the historians and archivists wrote in reply confirming what the ghosts had said to me. They really had been alive, and what they told me was true. After several years of such communications Walter presented his findings to fellow scientists at a conference in London whose conclusion was that this was good evidence to support the case that our personality does survive the death of the body. When word of all this became public, friends and local people suggested that I make use of this ability and invited my husband and me to accompany them on visits into haunted buildings to see if anything happened. When ghosts led us into fields, country paths and even woodland, we started to find their hidden or lost objects. But not every ghost leads to a 'find' as I call it. Most - like the ghost of the castle battlements - just want to off-load their skeleton-shaped guilty secrets.

CHAPTER TWO

NEWPORT
THE NOT-SO-GREAT ESCAPE

GHOSTLY WILLIAM was probably already present on the battlements when, in 1647, King Charles arrived, and must certainly have drifted along beside His Majesty on his small daily tour of the battlements' circumscription. Doubtless William was aware of the many misfortunes that so regularly confounded Charles' every attempt at escape. William must have relished the atmosphere of subterfuge and plot, delighted at such interesting times descending unto the dull days and nights of his lonely haunted castle, and royal company no less. He probably had even figured out the identity of the spies in Charles' network. As a man of some experience, he might have told the king exactly what to do with those who know too much; and perhaps he attempted to show him how. Not an arrow in the butt, just a helping hand at the back, in the dark, from on high.

Until one day, the king in the castle escaped. Well, almost.

Historians have long assumed Newport's name is etymologically self-evident - it was the *new* port for the lord of Carisbrooke Castle. But Victorian

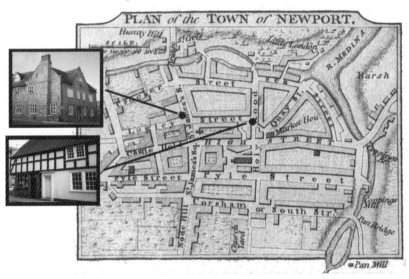

Newport's most haunted buildings. Old Grammar School (top) & Old Sun Inn

time-teamster Reverend Edmund Kell noticed Newport precisely fulfills all the criteria for being a Roman town; one indicator being the regularity of the plan on which this town is built. Streets form nearly a square and are crossed by intermediate streets at right angles. Kell suggested the town was built before AD 137, because a coin from the time of Emperor Hadrian was found enclosed in a stone wall in a house in the corn market.

Newport has some fascinating hauntings, for ghosts of all variety roam its venerable buildings and streets. Ghostly candlelight is seen at the windows of the Old Grammar school on St James' Street; nearby the Sun Inn building on Holyrood Street is the scene of terrifying supernatural dramas; and some people have encountered a sinister dark shape who stalks the old church yard area near Node Hill - now Church Litten park - where once stood the town's archery butts. There, bows long and short twanged and hummed and arrows split the target or not, depending, and doubtless someone or other went there one day and didn't come back alive. But the ghost of the park was nothing to do with that, nor was it a restless soul from the old burial ground below. The ghost of Church Litten park has been seen from time to time, and some local people will not walk there after dusk for fear of the dark shape that wafts the walkways and scares what little daylight remains in those who encounter her. I say 'her' because the park ghost was a woman, and

Church Litten park, near the old church yard, where a sinister dark figure is seen

9

when I saw her in the park one autumn evening she was dressed in a full long gown and wore a poke bonnet. Such high but dated fashion suggests she had been here for a good 200 years.

"... Can you hear me?" she said. Yes, I could, and had pencil and paper to record her words, as I always do. "I am haunting this area. It used to be a field that I crossed to go to the church from my home, if I chose to walk and not drive in the carriage. It was so long ago, I am bewildered by the change. Children used to jump out of the bushes and beg for farthings, nasty, dirty little things! I never gave them even a smile, let alone a coin.

One day a small ragged urchin stole my reticule. I had him caught and flogged in public. My husband was an important personage in this town. Alas, how it has all changed. No more floggings, no more respectable folk. All appear to dress like urchins, especially the women. Are there no ladies left?

I was responsible for children being flogged and an unmarried mother being driven from the town, branded a harlot. Once a gypsy girl actually touched my new dimity gown! I soon had her put behind bars. My word was listened to in Newport. My name is Elizabeth, a respected titled lady who roams now in distress. A path appears before me, due to you who puts my feet upon it. Can it be you? A rather untidy woman with no title or standing in the town? If it is, you have my gratitude. If not, forget it."

I have not attempted to identify the ghost of Church Litten park. I feel sure she would be horrified to find herself included in a book of ghostly rogues, though the presence of royalty in this collection might ease her disquiet. Perhaps her comments do illustrate how our definition of 'rogue' can change with the times; and doubtless her society circle would agree wholeheartedly that urchins who dare touch their betters deserve to be imprisoned, and that flogging children is a sensible thing to do.

*   *   *

The town's origins may date back into the mists of history but for many people Newport is probably most famous for the time when, in the autumn of 1648, it was the focus of world attention: it was here that King Charles I spent his final weeks of freedom, at the end of which a sad and desperate drama unfolded. The king had come to the Isle of Wight following defeat in the civil war. He had first surrendered to the Scots army, who then handed him back to parliament. Soon afterwards he was seized by Oliver

Cromwell's forces and held prisoner in Hampton Court palace, only then to escape. He headed for the south coast, passing Windsor Castle on the way, but avoided recapture by his enemies who had made it their HQ. He chose Carisbrooke Castle as sanctuary, but soon found himself imprisoned. Charles was consigned to solitary confinement for what his enemies considered to be betrayal of the country. Not only had he refused to accept parliament's terms of peace, but all the while he had schemed with and then against everyone, and then to crown all his scheming he had invited the Scots to invade England and come to his rescue. All his plans had failed, and no one wished to talk to him any more.

According to the diarist knight, Sir John Oglander of Nunwell, 1648 was the wettest year anyone could recall; but the quarter mile circuit of the castle's battlements was the only exercise Charles could get when he decided to come out of his room. To cheer his majesty in misery, gardeners from Newport helped lay a bowling green on the old place of arms, and a summer house was built in which to shelter from the rain. And some of them told how it was on the bowling-green that Charles learned the news that Oliver Cromwell was victorious; the Scots' forces had been pushed back across their border, and all his supporters who had rallied to his call to rise again for a second civil war were defeated, again.

'It is the worst news that ever came to England,' Charles is remembered for saying as he squelched over the castle's soaked lawn. 'If Cromwell had lost,' replied Governor Robert Hammond following Charles back from the tight collection around the jack, 'The Scots would now have the throne of

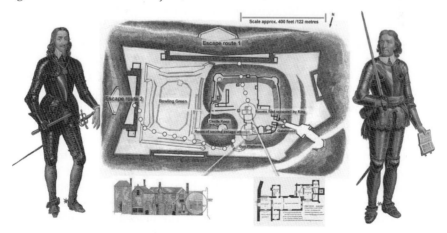

Charles I, Carisbrooke Castle plan, and Oliver Cromwell

11

England *and* Scotland.'

'I think not!' snipped the king, 'for I could command them back with the merest wave of my hand.' And with that said, the king turned, nosed the air then launched his last bowl across the green. Charles' final bowl plopped into the water-filled ditch. He wiped the raindrops from his nose and went to survey the damage. He stood and stared at the bobbing bowl, and then began to chew his lip as the cunning plan fomented in his head; while all those who watched, wondered if His Majesty had lost more than just the game of bowls out there on that wet and squelchy green.

'Perhaps it is time to think again about the Church,' said Charles, at last. 'Have parliament come to me and we shall talk treaty.' He fingered his wet beard, his mind thinking through the fiendish cleverness of the plan; he saw the gates of the castle open…It was so simple, why had he not thought of this before? He turned to the governor, 'But you cannot expect me to remain in here *imprisoned* while we do so.'

The governor was silent, wondering what the king had in mind by way of escape.

'I give you my word,' said Charles. 'I shall attempt no escape.'

The message was sent to London that King Charles would now consider discussing the terms parliament offered. In short, it was his surrender and parliament wanted the king's signature before Cromwell acquired it for the army, first.

Governor Hammond complied with parliament's orders to open the castle gates and release the king for the Newport Treaty meeting.

What followed was a bizarre conclusion to the king's fall from power.

THE HAUNTED HOUSE ON HOLYROOD STREET

Historians are divided over which building it was that King Charles chose to occupy during the treaty talks. Some say he remained in Carisbrooke Castle; others say he was found accommodation in a house in Holyrood Street. The Old Sun Inn building is one of Newport's most picturesque, with white and black timber work and diamond leaded windows; it is also one of the Isle of Wight's most notoriously haunted houses. The Sun Inn is not overly spacious, but it was crammed full of ghosts. A ghostly serving wench is often seen, and bloodstained clothing has been found; and in an attic room, a ghost with attitude has fun slamming doors and slapping guests. Some people say it is the ghost of frantic King Charles chewing his nails, fretting over plans for escape.

The first ghost to speak during my visit to the haunted house on Holyrood

Newport. The house on Holyrood Street, formerly the Sun Inn.

Street was a woman with a tragic tale to tell:

"... Thirty years of hell with the man I hated!" said she. "He raped me when I was but a girl, redeemed himself by marrying me, as I be with child. Yet, he made my life hell. He beat me and each time he came upon me at night it was like being raped over again. Hated him. Went to church like all the Christian folk of the town, yet my prayers for his death were never answered.

I tried so hard to live a decent life, bringing the children up well, but failed, as I killed him. Stabbed him one night with a kitchen knife through his heart, then ended me own life as would never face the gallows. I were a coward, yet it were me that became a ghost. Should have been him. No regrets. Me name is Margaret. Thank you for your help, you show me the way to the next world. Goodbye."

13

Multiple haunting is not uncommon, especially in old historic buildings. For the living, the dead can be no fun to share a house with, especially those with a grudge and a mean frame of mind. Some ghosts *do* have the ability to manipulate matter, some can move objects. Others have a more subtle influence by stirring up negativity and bad temper which when frayed by normal everyday problems can make things seem more gloomy and depressing. But in my opinion, poor Margaret the murderess, was not the malevolent 'poltergeist' of this Holyrood 'hell-house', though she had cause enough to rant from time to time and even take it out on the furniture. The second ghost was the more likely rogue for such activity. She actually managed to assault me with a scratch to the face and it was visible for several days afterwards; though she did express some remorse. Martha probably was responsible for the most frightening happenings in the Old Sun Inn, and the reason why no one living stayed for long in that building.

Various people of a doubting disposition told its residents their poltergeist problems would instantly disappear if they simply stopped believing in ghosts, that the slamming doors and frightening sounds would cease if they adopted a more scientific attitude; but such advice was useless, for it had no effect. This is a problem with ghosts: they will not go away even though some people dismiss them as mere creatures of folktale and Gothic fantasy. But in every country in our world there are people who have moved into a new home, who before that move never even gave the subject of ghosts a second thought, but having spent sleepless nights and tearful days, believe themselves to have a sitting tenant of the invisible kind.

One 'scientific' explanation recently offered for ghosts is that they are *atmospheric photographs*, products of emotionally-charged moments captured within the atmosphere of a site; an electromagnetic imprint that can replay what has happened before, to be glimpsed from time to time by a person sensitive or unlucky enough to pick up on it at the right moment. A good theory say others, but this cannot account for the most common ghostly encounter when, soon after death, a friend or relative appears to a witness as if they have come to say a last 'goodbye'.

To date, no one has managed to capture a 'live' ghost and persuade him or her to hold a press conference on prime time television; and so science mostly asserts there is no such thing as a ghost in the machine of the body to journey on after death or stick around to haunt the living. The majority of people in the modern world feel comfortable in accepting this, and instead of dwelling upon life after death, focus on the life ahead; which is sensible, wholesome and worthy. We should instead think of a new car, new house, a new career: things that are real. Until an advert pops up for funeral arrangements or life insurance and for a moment perhaps you and I wonder what happens when all we think we are, all we can feel and scratch and caress and pinch is dissolved into mud and sludge, or blowing in the wind in the crematorium garden. Is it merely wishful thinking to wonder if there is more to life than death?

And those people who, by lucky chance, survive accident or illness and wake up in their hospital bed to tell those nearest and dearest gathered with goodwill grapes and get well cards, of how they had a near-death experience in the ICU; of how he or she heard the beep of their flat-line state of death, but watched their own resuscitation from an unexpected 'second-person' perspective. They are told by those who think this cannot happen, that they had not become a temporary ghost, but were experiencing an hallucination. Sometimes curious survivors ask: '*How can a dead brain hallucinate?*' Only to be told such experiences are just the final transmissions of their consciousness, on facing its own oblivion. Exactly how long a mind may continue such transmission after death has not yet been measured in terms of seconds, minutes or hours.

These theories assure us that independent, walking, talking, door-opening, button-switching, object moving ghosts do not exist; it is the imagination of the living which credits the dead with this ability. And such reassurance is good and comforting, until in the middle of the night a ghostly figure wafts into your bedroom, screams and slaps your face, as has so often happened in the Old Sun Inn. But Martha, poor lost soul, couldn't help herself. It was something she just had to do:

"... My name is Martha, please set me free. I was a traitor to my master who was a titled gentleman, and to the king. Was a servant in this house. I received nothing but kindness here, which I repaid with evil gossip, causing misery to those who lived here and employed me. Ne'er a day went by after much sorrow. I regretted my wickedness. Tried to confess on my death-bed, yet no words came. Now have done more harm by marking you, who is kind enough to listen. I ask forgiveness as I go to be judged. Am released from this prison of guilt. Farewell."

I had time just to sharpen my pencil, before the ghostly Jack took over from Martha. How he managed this strong spirit ménage, is anyone's guess.

"... Used to run this place as a haven for tired men who needed a good tankard of ale away from the nagging of their women," said he with a sigh. "Knew all about females, married to a woman who was always cursing me and anyone who got in her way. I kept her away from serving. Had a handsome young fellow to help me, he could laugh with the men.

There were many stories told about this place, haunted they said. Some said it was a young man who roamed around lamenting for his lost lover. Others said it was King Charles who had been at the castle and who came here. But I did not believe in any of these stories. Why should any man haunt a place looking for any woman? They are all best left alone. And as for a king, why should he come here to stay? No such thing as ghosts. But what a mistake I made! Even blacked a man's eye in a row about the king. Would have none of that silly talk here. My wife said she had seen two ghosts, one man and one woman. I went to give her a beating but she just hit out at me and nagged all the more!

God left me here after I drew my last breath. Find myself talking to a woman who has a power to help me and does not nag me. Hard to believe. Jack's the name."

Then he was gone. The last of the Sun Inn's ghostly quartet knew something that was not so widely known; though what that secret was, will have to remain so for a little while longer. Or perhaps keeping a secret too long can drive you crazy:

"... We tried to keep it a secret, yet it seems we failed," he whispered. "The good folk here had left but methinks they left the ghosts of many behind. We tried so hard but it was still remembered. A great man had been here, a king, I tell you good mistress. A king to be hidden from memories of the folk of this town. One who was executed. Yea, I know. Me name is Richard, a name to be reckoned with, a great name.

The ghosts of so many roam this house. So different now. Ah! Wine from many parts of the world, ales it were afore that. Have been trapped by my lies. Keeping the secret so no one would be harmed as folk have long memories. I would have said "Long live the King!" I am leaving the secret behind. No one found the secret room which is no more. Thanks be to thee for helping me out of this place. The secret is out, cannot be kept."

This ghost's testimony may, or may not, contribute something useful to the debate over where King Charles stayed in Newport. Some historians believe the king was accommodated in an upstairs room in the Old Grammar School building in St James' Street, and not the Sun Inn.

16

Some also say the Treaty negotiations took place in the old town hall building not the Old Grammar school. But what *is* known for certain is that Parliament had granted Charles freedom to come and go as he pleased on the island so long as he stuck to his promise that he would not to try to escape while this Treaty was being negotiated, plus 20 days more. Parliament also agreed to restore some of his privileges and servants. Free in Newport Charles found old friends as well as new to look after him. In Carisbrooke Castle he was expected to break the ice in his own washing bowl, but Mary and Mrs Wheeler the laundry woman, were restored to do everything for him; and loyal Page of the Chamber, handsome Henry Firebrace. 'Majesty!' cried he, though soft enough so as no spies might hear, 'what plan of escape?'

Escape, of course, thought Charles; the town was a busy quay, the river Medina led to the sea; surely someone could find him a boat? Parliament's terms were unacceptable, but he might just persuade some commissioners to his cause. Or if it all came to nothing there was sweet Plan B - see out his parole and as the 20 days were over, Firebrace would give the signal and he would sail clear away out of Newport and out of the country. A boat was found and made ready.

Royalists and Roundheads came face to face in the streets and alehouses; ladies of the town came to visit His Majesty, but once only for those whose beauty spots were deemed 'too ambitious'; though it was difficult to avoid a mud-spattered addition to the face. As Sir John noted in his journal the town celebrations of Thanksgiving for the Army victories was a wet one. In fact 'It wase from morning to Nyght the horridist rayny Daye as ever I sawe, there wase almost no travelling on the Earth, both by reason of the flouds and Bogges in the high wayes that the rayne, and travelling made.'

September 18th, the parliamentary commissioners junketed in town while cannonballs whizzed harmlessly overhead in wet celebration of the honour of their presence; though not close enough to do useful damage, thought the king and Henry Firebrace. The Treaty house was made ready for the summit and orders were sent for the king to come from his lodgings.

What also is known is that during week three Charles wrote to loyal Sir William Hopkins who owned the house on Holyrood Street: '...I pray you give me an account as soone as you can,' quilled the king. 'First where I shall take Boate, how the tydes fals out? What Wynds are fair. Lose no time!'

For treaty-time was running out; question and counter question revealed to Charles that this was no negotiation, no discussion of terms, but complete submission of the King to Parliament's demands. His skillful replies and

Newport. The old Grammar School, St James's Street.

ripostes made not a dint in the commissioners' determination; not one of them was persuaded to agree his terms. He found himself conceding more and more to theirs. No compromise was offered. Charles thought of Plan B and scratched out another secret note to Hopkins: '…To be shorte, if I stay it will be too late to seeke a remedy. As you love my safety; let us dispatch this business as soone as we can. Believe me I am lost if I doe not Escape. For God's sake hasten!'

To this day there remains much mystery about how, why, where and when the great escape went wrong. The letters tell us the king was ready and there was a boat too in position. But no one knows for certain if the unlucky King of England had Hopkins' cunning plan in play, or that the fateful night unfolded due to the king's own noble but foolish fault, as dramatised by Sir Richard Worsley in his epic *History of the Isle of Wight*. But there may be more to it than what was recalled by the living. It may have been a sad miscalculation, as remembered by the dead.

Some locals believe it is the ghost of King Charles whose candle lights the Old Grammar School building, and that his sad spaniel eyes can sometimes be seen staring out from behind its windows. But the ghost of the old Grammar School was not the king.

Immediately on entering the building I felt the presence come toward me; accompanied by a sense of great despair and weary heaviness. It is true to say that ghosts are not always the bad, or the ugliest of rogues. Sometimes the good also need help to find their escape.

".... I pray you help me on," said the ghost of the Old Grammar School. "It was a terrible accident that hast kept me here. I was a loyal subject and loved the king. I served him well. It was in this place he handed me a letter to deliver to a friend who he said would help him. I swore I would do this small errand of mercy.

How could I lose such an important letter! Alas I did. Do not believe it was stolen. It was mine carelessness. I blamed myself as loved that man, who should never have met his death as he did. Alas I am still here, when I should have journeyed to heaven where surely he must be?

You, now mistress of the pen, are writing this down. Do not be as me and lose it. You help me onwards. I give you mine thanks. Me name matters not. You may think of me as John."

He called me 'Mistress of the pen' which may be a clue to his identity: for on the Isle of Wight there has only ever been one master - Sir John Oglander, friend of King Charles I.

CHAPTER THREE

QUARR ABBEY
THE WHITE FLOWERED COFFIN

G HOSTS come in countless different shapes and sizes, as do the living, which is not really a coincidence if you care to think about it. But there is another type of ghost, for which I have a description but not as yet an explanation. There *are* theories though, one of which suggests some of us live on in the thoughts of others in ways we could never have expected, even when those others are dead and buried.

Ghost-hunter T.C. Lethbridge came up with this idea to explain a ghostly encounter that happened to him. In 1959 T.C. found himself standing beneath a tree staring at an old mill when he noticed nearby a woman, and by the fashion of her clothes looked to be some 40 years behind the times. The ghost-hunter watched carefully and when a few moments later the figure vanished he then made some enquiries, only to discover that no woman remotely resembling the one seen had been anywhere near the mill at the time. 'I had seen what is known as a ghost,' said he. The encounter set him

Window, one of the few remains of old Quarr Abbey, Isle of Wight

searching for an explanation, and he came up with an answer that made sense to him: T.C. reasoned that ghosts are the products of emotionally-charged moments captured within the atmosphere of a site; electromagnetic imprints that can replay to those who are sensitive or unlucky enough to see them. Most modern theories of ghosts follow similar lines, describing them as *atmospheric photographs*.

Some in my experience *do* seem to be as T.C. described. I call these 'time-slips' but whether they are the result of someone else's perception, I do not know. One happens on the down-land near Niton, where a ghostly group of three ladies and two small girls appear, dressed in 1920s style. They seem to be busy looking for something. On one occasion I saw them so clearly. One lady wore a yellow dress and a long string of white beads. The second lady wore a white dress trimmed with scarlet around the neck and arm-holes. Around her head she wore a scarlet bandeau; and scarlet earrings dangled from her ears. The third lady wore a dress of blue with frilled cape-like sleeves; her hair plaited around her ears. The little girls were about eight years old, one in scarlet trimmed with white; and the other child wore a dress of white trimmed with blue. It looked as if they were going to a fancy-dress party. They did not look ghostly and yet that is what they were, for a moment later as I stood watching them, they disappeared.

But before they did so, I heard the ladies scolding the children for losing a china cup belonging to their grandmother. I told Walter who accompanied me that day, with our friend Carolyn, all I had seen and heard and we decided to look for the cup. We searched in the hedgerow and by bramble bushes but I felt drawn to an old gnarled tree; my companions followed me. We dug down into the earth and brought up a small pretty china cup. Unfortunately it was cracked on one side but otherwise in good condition. There was *proof* they had been there.

Had I witnessed a scene created by an upset child or angry parent? I do not know is the only answer I can give you; perhaps yes, perhaps no. Time-slips happen only occasionally and I can not make it happen at will. It just does. Generally I seem to be an invisible onlooker and for a few minutes in time I see and hear. On another occasion in a field near Strawberry Lane not far from the megalithic Longstone at Mottistone, I saw two men duelling with swords. I stopped to watch them; heard the sound of the metal clanging as their swords struck, and their rasping breaths as they tired. By their clothes I would identify them as from the 17th century.

Two of the most extraordinary of these time-slip events can be seen at the old Abbey of Quarr, on the north east of the island, and at Appuldurcombe house to the south; though what happens at Swainston Manor beats even

21

both of those, but I will come to that in due course.

I visited the old abbey with my friend Jenny Gibbons, we decided to walk to the ruins situated not far from the new one; on the way passing two monks clad in black habits. There is not much left to be seen of the original abbey, a few walls covered in lichen and ivy. Archaeological finds have surfaced at various times, a few coins and some other relics but not enough, say local historians and archaeologists, to throw much light upon the history of this abbey. On that day as I walked with Jenny toward it, for a brief moment the old abbey came back to life. At first I heard the sound of chanting, unmistakably of monks. Jenny too heard this, yet there was no one around, no one but us to be seen. A few yards further on I was impressed to turn around and at that moment saw a procession of monks dressed in brown, slowly walking in pairs behind a coffin being carried on the shoulders of monks. But what seized my attention was the coffin, for it was completely covered in white flowers. The procession then turned toward where the scant ruins now stand; the hedge we had looked over only minutes before was no longer there, it had vanished. The ruined abbey, as far as I could see, was fully restored. I whispered to Jenny telling her what was happening.

Unfortunately she did not see anything so clearly, but saw movement exactly where I had seen the monks walking in procession behind the coffin. Then the vision vanished.

Who was in the coffin; what memorable event was recorded at Quarr that day? Searching through archives in the local records office we came across the following account written in the 1600s by Sir John Oglander.

'At my first coming to inhabit in this Island Anno 1607 I went to Quarr,

Sir John Oglander

and inquired of diverse old men where the great church stood. There was but one, Father Pennie, a very old man, could give me any satisfaction; he told me he had been often in the church when it was standing, and told me what a goodly church it was; and further said that it stood to the southward of all the ruins, corn then growing where it stood. I hired some men to dig to see whether I might find the foundation but could not. He told me that it had a fair churchyard, and that the wall to the northward of the outmost south wall was but the outmost bound of the churchyard.

Now there is nothing left but ruins, except the cellar and buttery by which (as by Hercules' *foot) a man may judge for former greatness. The Abbot's private chapel is also now standing. Goodly monuments in the great church certainly there were, but those of chief note was Baldwyne Rivors, the first founder; Cicelye, the second daughter of Edward the fourth, who married for her second husband one Kyme, an Isle of Wight gentleman, a very proper man. She lived and died at East Standen, under St. George's Down, and the Lord Abbot desired that they might have the honour to have her interred in their church, which was performed with all honour and state by the convent and gentry of the whole Island, who attended the corpse from Standen to Quarr, where the Lord Abbot preached at her funeral.'*

The funeral cortege I had seen was of someone important that was certain, but was it for the abbey's founder 'Baldwyne Rivors', or Baldwin de Redvers, Lord of the Isle of Wight? King Henry I had given the island to the de Redvers family so unconditionally the crown had almost no authority here. Baldwin would probably have been the first big funeral event in the abbey but I did not feel the time-slip dated back quite so far, it didn't feel that 'old'.

I wondered if that funeral procession was for Princess Cecily. Although Sir John says she is buried here in Quarr, others say she was not; claiming she died on a trip to Herefordshire and was buried there. The fact there is no tomb here is thought to be proof she was not laid to rest in the Isle of Wight. But there are *no* tombs of any kind left to be found at Quarr Abbey. However, there *is* perhaps a clue to be found among its ghosts.

Princess Cecily was the second daughter of King Edward IV; born in March of 1469, in the palace of Westminster, she was sister to Elizabeth and Mary of York; her younger brothers were the two murdered 'Princes in the Tower'. In adult life she was first betrothed to James III of Scotland, though that did not happen. By lucky chance she avoided marriage to Richard III. She did marry Thomas Scrope, only to have this annulled by new King Henry Tudor who considered marrying her for himself, but instead chose eldest sister Elizabeth. In 1487 the king arranged for her to marry his Lancastrian kinsman John Welles, but that ended with his death.

Three years later, as Sir John notes, she married Thomas Kyme of the Isle of Wight, but the king was furious. She was banished from the royal court and everything she owned, all but the dress in which she was married, was confiscated; her children were excluded royal privileges. Cecily came to live on the island with her husband at East Standen house, where she died, says Sir John, in 1507 aged only 38 years. But without a tomb to confirm her burial at Quarr, Cecily's fate in death remains a mystery.

23

Funeral ceremony 15ᵗʰ century & King Henry VII, Henry Tudor

It is impossible to say for certain that what I saw was the funeral cortege of Princess Cecily of York. In H.G. Wells' book his time machine had a dial which indicated to which year he had arrived; but there is no such device in a time-slip. Of course during its long history many monks and abbots would have been buried in Quarr's churchyard; but how many I wonder, would have received the decorative addition of white flowers: all or none perhaps?

Or maybe the white flowers were the clue provided by the ghosts of old Quarr Abbey? They were rose petals, the white rose of York.

CHAPTER FOUR

APPULDURCOMBE HOUSE
THE POWER OF LOVE

URIOUSLY, ghosts of both variety live in this ruin. Appuldurcombe House now is unsafe for living flesh and blood to make its home, but for centuries it sheltered this island's most powerful and wealthy family. Royal favourites of kings and queens, the Worsleys were Knights and Captains of the Isle of Wight; military officers and members of Parliament; its heirs and daughters married into the very best of society.

However, its servants and local villagers envying such high status and wealth, consoled themselves by asking what good is power and prestige when you can be certain disaster will strike sooner rather than later? This great family prospered on the mainland but once here across the water things had a tragic way of turning out for the worse. Especially and mysteriously so for those bestowed with the name Richard, for these attracted even more bad luck than the rest.

Some islanders wondered if the ruination of this great house, and the affliction of its Richards, is linked to the destruction of Quarr Abbey. For of all the many houses of peace in Tudor England few were so badly damaged as Lord Baldwin's venerable abbey, so broken up and used for war. There are tales of love and hate within this ruin, for the fall of Appuldurcombe is

Appuldurcombe House, near Godshill, Isle of Wight

an epic told by those who try to guess the identity of its ghosts, and to which part of the tragedy they belong.

The drama begins brightly with courage and love. James Worsley won respect with the royal family for arguably the worst job in history: whipping boy for young Henry VIII, son of Henry Tudor. But when king, big Henry did not forget that favour: in 1517 he appointed him Captain of the Isle of Wight. He married lovely Ann Leigh, heiress to Appuldurcombe and the loving couple made the 'valley of the apples' their family home. In 1539 Henry decided to make a royal visit. Naturally he expected to be entertained with feasting and game-hunting in the abundant local woodland, trilling with fat pheasant and partridge; so fat they fell from the tree, even without the king's state-of-the-art gunsticks and powder, or so the game-keepers assured him.

Big Henry was love-sick and suffering over the death of his beloved third wife Jane Seymour. His minister Thomas Cromwell thought a trip to the island would be a tonic for the king, to ease his broken heart in sport. Not abroad, exactly but at least away from the mainland and all the moaning and groaning about his new policies for the poor since he closed down the religious houses, which in Henry's estimation were nothing more than hotbeds of lust and depravity, of vice and indolence; whose object of worship was money not God. Others thought this unfair and absurdly ironic.

Quarr Abbey was closed and broken; its venerable tombs of the de Redvers cracked open and plundered, its collection of medieval bones displaced; its monks cast out to live as best they could, and do what good they could for the poor. They, like the rest of the many displaced, were now at the mercy of Henry's laws for the poor. Bailiffs and officers were following Henry's newly upgraded laws, which in addition to whipping and ear-splitting now allowed for execution of any so-called 'valiant vagabonds' caught begging a third time. Public flogging and painful ear-splitting had been effective but not entirely the cure-all deterrent Henry and his accountants wanted.

Henry's laws offered the unemployed two options: work or death, though still preceded by a handsome whipping and torture for the good of public example. The joke amongst Henry's courtiers was how his laws had driven down the price of jesters; ex-priests taking to this profession were in demand due to that added God-forsaken look about them. Better they hop and jest and jangle, than lurk and loiter poaching in the woods. Henry's poor-laws aimed to stop the hunger-driven anarchy that was so irritating his noble landowners. Every man must be gainfully employed; and the nobles could expect no more loss of eggs and bird-life.

'You'll see, Majesty,' promised Captain James. 'Your laws have worked wonders on the Isle of Wight.'

Tudor Appuldurcombe House, with the beautiful people & the not-so-beautiful people circa 1530s

Sadly, Worsley died before he could show him but son Richard kept open the invitation to Henry. During the journey, Cromwell took the opportunity of healing his master's broken heart by telling the king of the lovely Anne of Cleves; and by the time they arrived Henry's heart was a-flutter with fleshy thoughts. Appuldurcombe's gardens were filled with his royal entourage, courtiers and minstrels, tents and grand spectacle. 'Splendid house, young Worsley,' grunted Henry. 'A fine party. Now for some sport...'

King Henry came, he saw but according to legend, he shot no bird-life. There was little to be had in all the forest. No pheasants' call; only the sound of distant giggling, and 'Ave Maria' sung in the woods. Henry's fury was matched by Worsley embarrassment. 'Poachers, Majesty,' was all he could say. And who knows if Quarr Abbey's lost Lord of Wight was at peace, for a few moments at least, in his unmarked hole in the ground.

MADAM BUTTERFLY

Appuldurcombe House is a good hunting place for ghost hunters, though how Lady Henrietta makes her curious combination possible is a fascinating mystery. The ghost of Lady Seymour Worsley was found haunting the ornamental Freemantle Gate; the ghost of Mary Targett, a dairymaid who gave birth to Captain Richard's love-child, haunted the house. The details of these cases can be found in another book, *Ghostly Encounters*, and need no repetition here; but there were what might be called 'common or garden' ghosts: those I most often encounter in my work, though Madam Butterfly might not appreciate that description, but we did find her in the garden. She is a typical example of what most ghosts are, and how they come to be in that state; what might be described as the more 'normal' paranormal: not time-slips of past events, but people trapped between dimensions.

We first found Mary in the front garden but when she spoke she led us south on a pathway toward Ventnor where she had lost a precious token of her love, as she explained to me one hot summer day. As always I had with me pencil and paper to record everything I heard. This is normally how I work: I find where the ghost is, and then I take out my notepad and pencil and let them talk. As they talk I write out in dictation what they have to say. It is simple, it is amazing, and it is fascinating; and that day accompanying me was a film-crew, who filmed the whole encounter.

Although she haunted the garden, perhaps there were occasions when the other Appuldurcombe ghosts took pity on her loneliness and invited Madam Butterfly into the house, and on quiet nights when the ghost-hunters were all gone, encouraged her to tell of the changing world outside; as they in return shared their secrets of how their beloved home became this ruin and yet remains a house of treasure.

For how long she had haunted the park she did not say but it was not so long as some ghosts, for she spoke of the house as a ruin.

"... He called me Madam Butterfly," said the ghost with a soft gentle voice, as I wrote what she said. "We met at a fancy dress ball. I was dressed as a Japanese lady. 'Very pretty', he said. We were very much in love, really love at first sight. Two weeks later we married by special license. He gave me a lovely keepsake to remind me of our first meeting.

We came to see the ruined house and eventually came here to have a picnic. It really was a lovely day. Then we continued our walk toward Ventnor. Over the stile I had to stop to fix my shoe. Sat to one side.

When I reached Ventnor I found that I had lost my keepsake. I was heartbroken and he a little annoyed. Never quite so in love after that. He only lived for six more months and I followed him a week later, as could not bear to live without him. I really loved him.

I saw my keepsake and stayed with it. I do not know whether you can find it. Over the stile, to your right, on a sort of rise. Do look, then you will prove I am real. You have now heard my story and I shall go on towards a light. My name is Mary. Thank you for listening to my rambling story. I *am* Madam Butterfly."

We did manage to find Madam Butterfly's keepsake. It was a small porcelain figure of a Japanese lady buried beside the path beyond the stile. Alas I cannot show it to you. That figure was immediately and quite rightly taken into the possession of the owners of the estate. But I hope they have not since thrown it away as being of little value, unloved.

THE FALL & CURIOUS RISE OF THE HOUSE OF WORSLEY

Inside two years of King Henry's visit, Cromwell was beheaded and Captain Richard Worsley was made Commissioner for the Sale of Church Plate. The 'Mauler of Monks' was gone, but 'Worsley the Fortifier', as he is known to history, now offered the island needy their options. But locals shook their heads and sighed in sad wonder that he was 'Worsley the Unlucky' when in 1567 his two sons were killed in a freak gunpowder explosion in the school house. Thereafter, his successors experienced a mostly unfortunate series of events. Sir Richard II lost an eye early in the 1600s, and nearly lost the other in a cushion fight. He next lost the love of his wife and then soon after, his life in a fight in Newport. Had cushions been the weapons of choice he might have stood a fighting chance. Even pulling down the old Tudor manor and replacing it with a new design did not offset the ill-fortune; though some might say that doom would not be doom if its course did not at first seem the sweetest option, and so Sir Richard 7th baronet, when offered the office of Governor of the Island, assumed he was at the height of an illustrious career and with the proposed marriage in 1775 to the lovely and deliciously wealthy Miss Seymour Fleming, he thought he had more than any man dare desire.

Following divorce seven years later, Sir Richard turned the family seat into a museum; a house of treasures. His collection of antique gems was breathtaking, so too his collection of pictures acquired during the French Revolution; but even these brought no happiness. Unfortunately far too many of those who came to view were heard to titter and snigger rather than gasp at the beauty of his collection; for no one could entirely remove from memory his wife's long list of lovers or his gardeners' knowing smiles. He moved out of the house and into a cottage near the sea. Sir Richard, third of that name and last of that line had lost everything: son, wife, career, reputation and will to continue the family name. But after his death in 1805 something extraordinary happened: the Worsley women discovered how a blighted house that so affects the living has no effect upon the dead.

Sir Richard's sister Henrietta inherited Appuldurcombe; her daughter Henrietta Anne's marriage to Charles Pelham, Earl of Yarborough, brought it all into his possession; but, unexpectedly, something else came with it. 'Upon opening the doors,' wrote Wyndham after visiting Yarborough's lucky inheritance, 'it disclosed such a variety of beauties as made us forget all criticism. Whichever way we turned our eyes, the most precious pieces of ancient sculpture, and paintings of the Roman and Venetian schools claimed our attention.' Every room superbly furnished and decorated with fine pictures and outstanding drawings of cities, countries and ruins of the East, '...nothing spurious or like the refuse of other collections,' observed Wyndham. Pride of place were originals of queens Mary and Elizabeth I, kings Henry VIII and Edward VI, gifts to the Worsleys from those in the picture.

Yarborough is fondly remembered as a generous man who maintained a splendid hospitality at Appuldurcombe. Founder and first commodore of the Royal Yacht Squadron, locals noted with special sadness how he died, 'somewhat suddenly' in September 1846, aged only 55. The second Earl Yarborough did some work on the house and rearranged the library to please his wife, and then in 1855 decided to sell. The museum contents were put up for auction together with house and grounds. Finest of its pictures were taken up to London for display in the Yarborough's home and by 1857 the last of Captain Worsley's family was gone from Appuldurcombe.

There was no one left to note the happy discovery within only weeks of their departure, of three missing bodies found at Quarr Abbey. By strange coincidence after some 300 years lost, Lord Baldwin, his wife and son had surfaced. But even then, it seemed, the vengeance of the lost lord was not complete. The house was purchased and turned into a college for gentlemen; then it became a temporary home for Benedictine monks here to build a new abbey in Quarr. Then, during World War II when the house was used as a billet for soldiers, a bomb blew out its roof and windows and with them, all hope of restoration. Appuldurcombe House is now a shell, but this is perhaps the way its ghosts want it to appear to us, the living. One ghost is named Henrietta and for her this is not a ruin, but a house of love. I call her 'lady' and she seems not to mind. She is quite friendly and I often see her in the library.

Once I glimpsed the room as it was: warm and inviting with velvet curtains, beautiful carpets and bookcases full of leather-bound books. On

Appuldurcombe House, the library

that occasion Lady Henrietta came close enough to show me the book she was reading, Chaucer's *Canterbury Tales*. She held it open at *The Miller's Tale*. Another time, I saw her playing a spinet and that day she wore a different coloured gown. Each time I ask if she wants help to leave, but each time she always politely refuses. Lady Henrietta may tell you that it is not so bad being a ghost.

Many people say we cannot take possessions with us when we die, but it seems that we can, although there is a price to pay. To be more precise: our possessions can carry *us with them*. Some ghosts' fate is to accompany a valued possession or object, Mary 'Madam Butterfly' for example. But Lady Henrietta has achieved so much more, not only is she still resident in Appuldurcombe House, it remains as it was, complete with library, books, spinet and clothes. I am not the only witness to have seen this; others have as well, which raises the question: if different people independent of each other see the same thing, that too must be a reality.

Often it is said we cannot take what we love of this world into the next, but it seems we can take enough into the past; so long as we journey with it. That is the price. Thus Sir Richard's house of treasure is here, even though it may not be so immediately apparent to us the living.

Sir Richard might say that love built his family's dynasty and then brought it crashing down. Lady Henrietta and her ghostly partner remind us all that love can also keep the impossible together.

31

CHAPTER FIVE

THE ROYAL YACHT SQUADRON
MURDER MYSTERY

THE WORLD FAMOUS Royal Yacht Squadron, focus of Cowes Week sailing regattas, stands on the foundations of a Tudor gun fort; one of those built to defend against marauding French raiding missions. But now each Cowes Week welcomes French and Spanish sailors as the world's finest yachts-people come here to mingle with incoming tides of VIP merry-makers; though some of these have not impressed the class-conscious ghost haunting the building's upstairs rooms. Downstairs in the kitchen, staff have feared a knife-drawer rattling poltergeist in their basement realm. The Royal Yacht Squadron was haunted by two ghosts, each with murder in mind.

For centuries Cowes played a vital part in the defence of this nation and Britain's seafaring fortunes; ship-building and sail-making have brought great fame and prosperity to the island and even long after a vessel was launched, popping corks and good cheer continued. Indeed, the Isle of Wight has a rich history of merriment, though excess was curbed for a time during the mid 1600s following defeat of King Charles in the civil war. But nothing can remove from memory the merry times of mad Lord Portland, governor of the isle. His blast-and-get-plastered parties were legendary. During late summer of 1639, diarist knight Sir John Oglander noted the governor's party

Royal Yacht Squadron, Cowes Castle

32

capers, of how he and all his lordship's friends: '…drank and shot, shot and drank till they were scarce compos mentis,' said Sir John. 'I may truly say that in the space of six days there was never so much powder fired except against an enemy. Friday the 2nd September they all drank, they were all madd, at every health tearinge of one another's Bandes and shirtes insomuch as linnen was very hard to be found amongst them.'

Unfortunately, Lord Portland was imprisoned for such 'acts of jollity' and following his arrest in August 1642 the people of Cowes watched the menacing maneuvering out on the Solent. As Paul Hooper describes in the excellent *"Our Island" In War and Commonwealth*, Parliament ordered a blockade of loyalist Portsmouth dockyard; one of the blockading ships - the *Lion* - standing off Cowes fired on two boats from the island bound for Portsmouth. Humphrey Turney, who commanded Cowes Castle, fired upon the *Lion*. It was among the first shots fired in the civil war. In response Captain Dick stormed ashore from the *Lion*, arrested brave Turney and seized the castle in the name of Parliament. By the wet autumn of 1647 hapless King Charles I arrived at Cowes on his way to Carisbrooke, where he spent his last year before execution.

Some people claim it is Turney's ghost who roams the battlements to this day, haunting through weather fair and foul, ready with burning match and eyes on the Solent; though others say they saw the ghost of a woman in the clubhouse rooms.

One afternoon I was invited into the Royal Yacht Squadron. In the cramped office the Secretary sat at his desk and gazed at me as though through the eyes of a drowning man, and explained how kitchen staff were being scared by a ghost fooling around with the contents of the knife drawers. He did his best to take on board the possibility that ghosts do exist, smiled politely then led me downstairs to the below world of the castle. The kitchen was quiet, with no sailing events that day; but when there were, we can wonder whether Matthew the ghost contributed to those big occasions in his own unique way. I am sure those who have been troubled by his presence will be glad to know he now has left the building. Matthew confessed at long last to a secret murder; for there is quite literally a body in the basement, hidden in the foundations of the Royal Yacht Squadron.

"… In torment and in agony my spirit has tarried by the foundations I built," he complained. "By the holy rood joyful tidings come to me. Knoweth I that thou canst send me thither to paradise.

Into a dusky tomb mine enemy was placed. A plague upon him, he required speedy payment or forfeit my life. A blow upon his head, stones put upon him, his flesh long gone, his bones now dust. Many crowns I owed this worthy soul, so took the path of violence. His absence was noted not. High seas could bear the guilt. Thou cometh and dare Matthew hope for paradise after endless years?

Fare thee well stranger, I go. His dusty bones remain in the foundation, his soul has long gone on."

Matthew from the lower levels was not the only ghost with murder in mind; so too had a ghost from 'above'. I found her haunting an upstairs room. She did tell me her name, a noble no less; she offered me a coin for my trouble and confessed to a similar crime, albeit accidental. It may perhaps be possible to check back through the records to confirm that someone at the Yacht Squadron met with a tragic end on dry land. It may be possible to confirm the murderess was there that very day. But would it do either any good? Sometimes it is better not to know.

"… I thought you were leaving," she chided. I grabbed my pencil and paper to record her words. "I came here many years ago when it was first opened as a yacht club. Oh, the grand times we had sitting watching the yachts. My husband sailed, I feared the water, preferred to remain as spectator. The clothes were more acceptable to me than the yachts. Royalty often graced this building, and still does. Yet royalty is not like it was, far too free with the language. It shocks one such as myself, a born lady.

I fear I behaved in a manner not befitting my station in life, drank too much champagne, it always changed my nature. Going to the room set aside for lady guests I struck a servant girl such a blow she fell, striking her head on a heavy oak chair. I saw she was dead. I withdrew. No one was around. Too busy with their champagne and talking about the last race. We did not hear about the accident, it was only a maidservant. But when I died, I found I was trapped by guilt, a murderess. You, a woman of no title and no reason to be here, can release me, sending me to meet whoever there is to greet me. My name is Lady F. Thank you. If I had a coin I would give it to you for your trouble. Murderess I may be, but I was not mean."

The ghostly Lady F. no longer haunts the Royal Yacht Squadron, and murderous Matthew too is gone, though his victim's dust may still be found in the nooks and crannies. But where now they have gone is anyone's guess. Life is complicated, but so too is death, it would seem, so those ghosts who came to my house informed me.

CHAPTER SIX

INTO THE MIST

THERE IS ANOTHER VARIETY of ghost, whose existence raises even more mysterious questions than answers. Among this type - and so far to date - I have encountered no royals but I certainly found a pair of rogues. Smuggler, turned horse-thief and burglar, Stephen Diprose was one of these. He was not a time-slip; he was not stuck haunting somewhere in the Isle of Wight, but where he came from, and how he managed to travel, is a mystery.

He gave a grotesquely fascinating description of how his life came to an end on the gibbet. His death also confirms the 'drifting out of the body' event that so many people, who have had near-death experiences, or N.D.Es, describe. He came to my home, and over a period of several hours told me the short story of his life. It did not take him all that long, it's just that these types of ghosts come and go. It seems either they do not have the power or energy to travel and converse, or I to listen, for any considerable duration. They talk in short bursts and then come back an hour or so later, sometimes the next day. How or why this is, I don't know.

Perhaps it was inevitable that he would find his way to the hangman's noose. He did have warning of his doom, cryptic though it was to him, but you don't have to be psychic to figure out what it meant.

"… Life as I knew it were taking things and selling 'em or drinking the good old brandy we brought up from beaches," said he. "Plenty of barrels we got from different beaches along the Kent coast. I were just one of the men who rolled barrels into hiding from customs men. Me family before me did the same, a rare sport it were to keep out of sight of the customs man. Men getting hung for smuggling, had to be careful. Stephen my name. Saw one of the men swinging from the gibbet. He was unlucky. I very sure of myself, but sometimes scared in case I got caught.

Cannot do any more with smuggling, too many men now taken and swinging on gibbets, left for all to see as warning. Only way is to rob. Not got horse, find a better way.

Terrible when I was caught at High Halden. The man was a half-wit, where money was I forced him to tell. Always a way, 'specially if there is a woman around.

I got to taking anything I could lay my hands on after I finished with the smuggling. Several purses I took betwixt stealing a sheep and a fat goose which made a dinner for a sennight. Then some clouts from a washerwoman and a horse that I tried to sell but had trouble. The wenches did not want to bed with me unless there were some siller for 'em. One of 'em I swear was a witch, she had eyes yellow like a cat and could lay a man and make him think he were in paradise. Was the women like her that made me do it. Always 'fraid of the gibbet. The witch woman said, 'Beware of maid with stone'. So every time I saw some wench working in a field I stayed far from her for she may touch a stone. If some woman wore a ring with a stone in it I would not steal it, or even rob her. But at the court they sent me to Maidstone. The witch was right, damn her!

Plague take the cully at Rochester who sent me to swing on the gibbet, to be left till crows pick the flesh from me bones, hanging in chains. A warning, he said, for others to lead a better life than me. Plague take the damned cully. Horse-stealing he said was a bad thing, but to threaten honest men and women in their homes 'e said. All right for 'im who has always had a warm bed and food in 'is belly.

May God help me. Was it me I was looking at? I was dead, dead, dead! They had put the damn noose round my neck, a jerk and I knew I was dying. The choking pain! And then the tunnel. The tunnel. Down, down, down, and mist forever. Was it damned mist forever, was this death? I saw myself hanging on the gibbet. No, not me, God! Take the man who sent me. It was me I looked like. Ah, ah! My tongue was hanging out like a long red rag. Then more mist, mist got blacker, could not see anything. Help me! Black, black mist. Just a little light but mostly mist, damned mist."

Without a surname it seemed impossible to confirm this man's identity but Walter, my husband, made the most of what information I had been given. He told me his name was Stephen and spoke of smuggling in the county of Kent, but had been caught robbing a house in High Halden. He was tried at Rochester and was sent to Maidstone. High Halden is a village between the towns of Ashford and Tenterden in Kent, but there would be no useful records there. Rochester, on the river Medway, is the nearest city; Maidstone is the county town of Kent, and location of the county prison.

Walter first searched the Maidstone prison archives for any execution of a robber named Stephen, sent there from Rochester. Records date back to the early 1800s when the prison was constructed and 58 executions are documented. Some people were hanged inside the prison, others outside the main gate. Walter read the grim list; the majority of people were hanged for

Sample of Margo's automatic writing, as dictated by a ghost murder; a few for rape and arson, an unlucky highwayman and one man executed for sodomy. 'No burglars hanged at Maidstone,' said Walter. 'No one named Stephen. That's all I can find.'

Had it been my imagination, I wondered? Walter contacted the local newspaper in Maidstone seeking information about executions prior to the construction of Maidstone prison, and several days later he received an answer that for centuries before, executions for all criminal offences were carried out on nearby Penenden Heath. The assizes - the periodical sittings of judges on the county circuit - were held at Rochester for Lent and summer in the years 1737 to 1741 and 1743 to 1748. There were only Lent assizes in Rochester in 1735, 1749; 1753 to 1764 and in 1773. All other years the assizes were held in Maidstone. Walter searched the Rochester assize records, there were Williams and Henrys; Thomases and Johns and Richards aplenty, but only three Stephens: Stephen Potts, hanged at Penenden Heath for the murder of Jesse Taunton on 28th March 1799; and one Stephen Diaper, hanged for murder in 1739. And there, in the assize entry for Monday 6th March, was Stephen Diprose, hanged on Thursday 30th March 1749 at Penenden Heath near Maidstone, "for robbery in a dwelling house".

Stephen Diprose was one of many ghostly individuals who came to my home to talk, and I include some of these other cases in the book *Heaven & Hell*, for this is an issue related to that title, more so than *Royalty & Rogues*.

He was not the only one to tell me how after death he ended-up stuck in some form of disorientating misty existence. He and all the others clearly retained a sense of who they were, and of the details of their life but it is difficult to picture such an uncomfortable state of being. I so often think it bad enough haunting a building, but just to be adrift in mist must be really uncomfortable; lost in mist for a hundred years or more. In one sense this may explain where he had been all that time, but it does not answer *where* that mist exists.

THE LOCK-KEEPER'S SECRET

John Cannon was another ghost who came to speak to me in my home. He believed that soon after he died he had been deliberately pushed into a mist from which he could not escape. He was quietly spoken when first he made contact but towards the end his voice became stronger as if he really was clawing his way out. At first there seemed no record of his existence. After writing letters to various archives we had nearly given up trying to prove his life, but persistence paid off as Walter's research eventually uncovered a book listing lock-keepers on the river Thames. The old rare book mentioned the lock on the Kennett, gave names and dates, listing a John Cannon who lived in the lock-keeper's cottage between 1825 and 1827. This is what he told me of an incident which so affected his life, and his death.

"… 1825 to 1827, lock-keeper, had a house, lovely little house. 1827 went through the tunnel of death to bright light. Fifty shillings a month I received and the lock house was the nicest home my wife and I had. But only two years, and then was lost. Now I can get to your hand.

The summers were pleasant, the grass grew tall. In my time between duties I tended my garden, the currant bushes bore fruit and my good wife made jam. The smell of jam-making was a thing that meant a lot to me but there was a woman, younger than me, comely, with bold eyes. Any man she would talk to and oft spoke to me, and would have been more for the taking. But had no time for the likes of her. May I be forgiven for what was to happen. I am so grateful I have found your hand to hold on to and to tell my troubles. You will help me, please, please, please help!

Blue lights, green lights, yellow and white lights, and I took the wrong light which led to grey mist. Help me to get from the mist. I heard voices and someone pushed me through to you. I know not who helped me to get to the right light.

The comely woman would not leave me be. I even told my dear wife but she said much as she loved me, how could such a wench want a man as I, when such handsome younger bucks and village lads were seeking such as she? Then one day I was out in the field by the path, I saw her. Help me."

Then he was silent. I wanted to help, if that was possible. I sensed he had not finished but felt the cold presence drift away and then was gone. I waited but heard nothing more until later that evening. He returned and when he did so his voice sounded clearer and closer.

"Still in grey mist, help me! My name is John, for two years lock-keeper. The woman was alone and quite bare from the waist up. She came up to me, 'I lost my bodice when washing in the river.' I told her I would fetch my wife, and the woman did not look pleased. My wife gave her a shawl to cover herself with and she left promising to return it next day. As I walked down the towpath later I saw her bodice on a bush. I knew she had put it there and not lost it. The grey mist is getting less all the time. The woman did not come for a sennight and then I came home from a long walk to find her with my wife, having a posset, as it was a cold day.

The Thames and the Kennett had looked so clear with the frost on the grass and leaves. Help me from the mist.

The woman suffered from some evil humours that caused her to behave strangely when the moon was full, my wife told me, and that was why she threw off her clothing. It was the evil in her taking over. We saw her oft after that visit but in the February she became a nuisance, and when she slipped on the riverbank I stood and watched her without going to her assistance. The pretty countryside around me would be a prettier place without her.

The mad woman had fallen so that the lower part of her body was in the water, and she lay very still. I took no notice, it was very near the village of Sonning and I returned home without another glance at her. Someone would find her from the village.

The next day everyone was talking about her. She was found by a girl and boy who were courting and she had been taken to her hovel. One of her strange ways was on her, as it was full moon, but then I heard she had some trouble breathing as laying so long in the wintry weather had not done her anything but harm. I felt bad about it, but said nothing. I had thought that as her head and shoulders were not in the water she would come to no harm. But I was wrong.

There is a little light in the grey mist now. I can see lights, lovely lights. It is your hand that has pushed the mist away and I can go on now to another life, I know not where but the mist has gone. The woman died, I was sorry as although I did not want her around me I should not have left her where she was.

It was some months after, I too went down the tunnel of death. I felt she pushed me to the grey mist. My dear wife grieved for me but I knew she had a home to live in and would not be turned out. The grey mist has nearly gone. The bright light is lifting me I know not where, but now feel happy out of the mist. "

Then lock-keeper John Cannon spoke no more.

THE DIAMOND RING

So why is it that some ghosts get stuck on castle battlements, or in parks or houses, while others are free to go to visit psychics in their home? The answer to that is: I do not know; all I can tell you is what they tell me. Is it better to be free-floating in an endless mist, or 'anchored' somewhere? If it is somewhere familiar, perhaps they are luckier than those stuck in the middle of nowhere, like Jim and Rose, two ghost rogues attached to lost objects of desire.

I try, but it is sometimes difficult to be non-judgmental when hearing of the cruelty people inflict upon the vulnerable whom they claim to love and care for. Those private moments of temptation that come to us all at some time or another, when a choice must be made; these are more important than perhaps we realise, for these are the truest tests of character: when we think we are alone and no one is watching. And sometimes I cannot help but wonder what would have happened if some of the dead had been united in life. Olive's man Jim, for example; a good thing for him perhaps that he had not got himself hitched to Rose, the murderess. Meanness is a bad trait in anyone's character, but to deceive a blind person who loves you is deplorable. This next case is about such a man. We found Jim the ghost at a place named Gun Hill by a country path leading to Atherfield. Walter and I had set off with another willing friend, Louise. We had nearly a mile to walk along the country lane rich in ripe blackberries, and we soon were discussing the making of bramble jelly and blackberry wine. I had almost forgotten that I had important work to do, when a man's voice broke into our conversation, and I grabbed pencil and paper. I could feel him close, the other two stood silent and watched as I listened to what he said.

"… How could anyone be as cruel and mean as I was? I met Olive at work and I never really loved her, she wore thick glasses as her sight was failing. She knew she was going blind and would one day be in a home, as she had no relations.

I wished for companionship and a woman. I was not exactly handsome as I had a bad birthmark on my face. We were to be engaged and I thought seriously that if I spent pounds on a ring it would be a waste, as she could not see the ring properly. So I brought an imitation diamond ring. She tried to look at it through her dimming vision and thought she had the real thing. She went completely blind a year later, and then when she died I came on holiday walking on the island. I had the ring as it was on my conscience. It was not only that but other mean things I did, just because she could not see. It was no excuse for meanness. I came along here and as I fumbled in my pocket I realised I had dropped it through a hole, it must have been as I climbed the gate. I keep seeking for it. My meanness keeps me in a cloud of mist alone, searching. Oh Olive! Why was I so mean?"

We were standing near a gate, so first by one post then the other we dug in

Jim's ring for Olive

search of the ring. After a time we concentrated our efforts in the middle of the pathway but somehow I felt pushed to one side by unseen hands, and I let the ghost lead me, with Walter and Louise following. Then down on our knees digging and clawing away at the damp earth and grass; I saw a faint light appear around Louise's hand and within a few seconds she unearthed a very muddy ring. We cleaned it as best we could and at first sight it looked like real gold and diamonds, but on closer investigation it was obviously a fake. "What a mean man," we all remarked; then I sat back knowing I would hear his voice again and my faith was soon justified.

> "To be denied the sight that normal folk have. To be denied beauty and a good figure, and to be denied a husband who was normal looking was a great burden for Olive. But to be denied the decent things that I could afford was a terrible sin, it was cruel of me.
>
> I was not the best-tempered person. Although poor Olive did her best, as being blind the house was not always kept as clean as I would have wished it. Is it a wonder that I have been trapped here? But forgiveness is given now. I can hear Olive's voice calling me, I am straining to catch the words, "Jim, it does not matter, come to the light. I can help with the assistance of another lady who spirals around the lady who writes." I shall go on now and leave the mist, trying to make up for my mean nature."

42

THE FINGER TREE

A good thing for Jim he wasn't attracted to Rose, a lady who believed in superstitions. Her story, although tragic in one sense, has made many people smile when it has been told to them, so I feel I have to include her case in this book. We found her haunting the woods near Calbourne, on the way to Yarmouth town. Arrangements were made with Doreen, a lady who had been on many rescue outings with me, to pick up Walter and me. Upon reaching Calbourne we began walking up a rough stony track through dense woods. We had gone about a quarter of a mile when I sensed the presence of this ghost. We sat and within a few minutes she spoke and I scribbled down all she said. Like Jim, Rose was keen to talk about what was on her mind.

"… Rose is my name," said she, "and I rose from poverty upwards, but now I am so low. When I tell you what I did you may not wish to help me. I was a country girl, my father was a farm labourer. I had three men who wanted to marry me, I just could not make up my mind. 'Get each one to buy a mustard spoon and take the spoons deep into the woods,' granny told me. 'Bury them and leave them for two or three months and then dig them up, the one that is most shiny, marry, as he will rise.'

I did that and married Henry, he became quite comfortably off as he had several strokes of good luck. After a few years I was unhappy with him and I had the opportunity to send him on his way. So I took it. He was ill with feverish cold and took to his bed. The east wind was very cold, I opened the window and put damp sheets on the bed and he was dead within five days. I then sat back and enjoyed the insurance money. After a few years I became bored and needed a man. There were many after me, as I was a handsome woman, big and healthy, with masses of hair. I chose three again for the mustard spoon superstition. I went into the woods and buried them behind where you are sitting. Soon after, I became ill and died before the time came to dig them up. You can find them and help me, if you will be kind. Or do you hate me and condemn me as a murderess, and leave me to linger here?

Ten paces to the side, ten forward facing the woods and ten to the side and look near a finger tree. Help me, please!"

After I had read Rose's message to Doreen and Walter we started our search for the mustard spoons. Our first question was what is a 'finger tree'? We had no idea; and the length of our paces was different. We got caught in brambles, then stung by nettles and our hair pulled by low branches. We did

43

Rose's lost mustard spoons, though one is perhaps for salt

not know whether she meant the right or left side, but eventually I noticed a tree stump with thin shoots growing straight up from the centre of the stump, like fingers. We all started to dig around it. Then a cry from Doreen, "I've found one!" she was holding up a tarnished mustard spoon. Then Walter dug another out of the ground a few centimetres away. Finally I found the third on the other side of the stump. How strange we must have appeared, three very untidy people, each holding up an old tarnished spoon. We made our way back to where we had been sitting, praying she would be released from being earthbound; and then her soft country voice sounded in my ear.

> "I am so pleased my instructions were not in vain. We always called sprouting tree stumps finger trees. I was wicked, as Henry was a good man, just dull at times. I had no children, I would have liked a little girl, but it was not to be. No one remembers these country superstitions anymore. Thank you for helping me, wicked though I was. I see a silver of such brightness, better than a new spoon. I am going towards it as it is lovely and comforting."

I wonder how many people have heard of this method of choosing a husband? I cannot imagine a young lady in this day and age going to this trouble. Belief in this superstition gained Rose a wealthy husband, although obviously she was not contented. She is now released and haunts those dark woods no longer.

44

Ghostly rogues like Rose and Jim, Stephen and John were relatively easy to find, but royalty? None came to speak to me; and there was no sign of the ghost of Henry VIII haunting Appuldurcombe House, but in my opinion it was unlikely he would be there; though in truth I think few ghosts are able to choose their location to haunt. It just happens, somehow, though Lady Henrietta is lucky indeed to get what she wants, but probably might not be so happy if big Henry the phantom king was roaming her home.

Royalists might believe that Henry's absence from Appuldurcombe, and King Charles I not haunting Carisbrooke Castle or the Old Grammar School had nothing to do with location or connection, it is simply because royals do not suffer the indignity of becoming a 'common' ghost. Henry and Charles may have assumed this to be true, being God's chosen 'lieutenants on earth'; like the great pharaohs of ancient Egypt, they would, by Divine Right, expect to be on the fast-track to heaven. Who knows how many people believe there is a special access door for those born into a royal family?

Is there a good reason why a ghost cannot be a royal, or a royal become a ghost? (Incidentally, I am not especially royalist or republican-minded.) Or is it a matter of location and connection of some significant sort? If so, there is a chance that anywhere can have its own royal resident of a supernatural kind, though any possibility of the Isle of Wight hosting a royal ghost would be limited to the venues they have visited, just like anyone else. Henry VIII came to Appuldurcombe; according to legend King William the Conqueror, in 1082 was at Carisbrooke Castle confronting brother Odo, the bad bishop of Bayeux. There is also a dubious legend that wily King John hid in a wooded creek near East Cowes for three months, after signing Magna Carta.

I doubted we would find a lost royal haunting the Isle of Wight woodlands. Historical documents confirm a visit by King Edward I, to Swainston Manor during the autumn of 1285; and King Henry VII, so diarist knight Sir John Oglander notes, spent a week at Carisbrooke Castle. King James I made two visits; whereas his unlucky son Charles stayed a year, and grand-daughter Princess Elizabeth, only a matter of days before she died there. More recently, in the 1800s, Queen Victoria moved into Osborne House in East Cowes and made it her island home.

It would be lucky indeed to find the Conqueror haunting old Carisbrooke Castle; nor did I find kings Henry Tudor or James I. Perhaps more likely, King Charles, or little Elizabeth, but neither were there.

Perhaps it *is* because royalty is spared the queue for heaven.

Or maybe it is about the *connection*, but how strong must it be?

CHAPTER SEVEN

YARMOUTH CASTLE
THE GHOST GUNNER'S WOE

COUNTRY GHOSTS probably get less opportunity to spook the living than those in historic public buildings; but this does not necessarily offer greater satisfaction. Hal, the ghost of Yarmouth Castle, could tell you about that particular frustration. Yarmouth Castle is a castle in a town with a history of danger. For until relatively recent times the inhabitants of the Isle of Wight considered their home to be a dangerous frontier land. Invaders inevitably used the island as a base from which to launch attacks on the mainland. The raids became especially irksome following King Edward III's military sortie into France in 1348. That mission so enraged the French, they declared it as just and right to sail across the Channel to pillage and ruin as much of England as they could, in short-breaks of entertainment.

In 1377 the huge war fleet filled to bursting with excited soldiers sailed for England. French knights and Spanish seamen roamed the English coast burning and looting as many seaports as they could. They landed on the island and destroyed its principal towns; but lost their commander to a well-aimed arrow at Carisbrooke. But Yarmouth town was burning; its people groaned for mercy while the French demanded 1000 marks to go away. They were paid, and they did go but in 1541 they returned with an even bigger force. They crashed ashore from the French warships and this time they also carried away Yarmouth's church bells. That such horror may never revisit,

Yarmouth town, Isle of Wight with church on left and castle centre

the townsfolk begged King Henry VIII to build a gun-fort; for everyone knew what to expect when the last enemy seaman, before splashing aboard his boat, wiped his whiskers and sneered, 'We'll be back.' Henry agreed, but too late, for the French returned with a vast invasion fleet carrying enough men and weapons to invade all of England. While they waited for Henry's navy to come out of Portsmouth harbour and be annihilated on that hot, windless afternoon in the summer of 1544, some of them rowed on to Yarmouth and burned it to the ground.

'Guns there!' roared Henry, when at last they were gone, leaving only the memory of their shrieking laughter as his beloved warship the *Mary Rose* had rolled over and sunk, to the sound of splash, splutter and foul-mouthed recrimination. 'And guns there in Yarmouth!' Henry roared again. 'Guns everywhere! Blast the Frenchies!'

Yarmouth Castle was to be the most modern of its kind, built amid the ruins of the village church, and built from the stone of Beaulieu Abbey. A new fortress design was chosen: an arrow-headed bastion and recessed gun ports. By 1559 there was one gunner housed here, but it is claimed he saw no action. Nor the 70 gunners during the Dutch wars of the 17th century; and during the civil war its royalist captain surrendered the castle to the parliamentarian forces. But Hal, the ghostly gunner of Yarmouth Castle, would never surrender; and by the sound of things he had seen action somewhere.

Records confirm the castle was still garrisoned in 1781 by a captain, a master gunner and five other gunners. During the following years its defences and weapons were upgraded as technology changed, until 1885 when the garrison was withdrawn and the guns dismantled. From then onward the ghost of Yarmouth Castle was bereft of living company, until the 1900s when soldiers were billeted here during the two World Wars. As if Hitler's forces weren't enough to trouble those soldiers' dreams, there was ghostly Hal in the castle, drifting through its walls and into their nightmares, scaring them with his constant muttered complaints of conditions; of which he told me during a visit to his castle. I found him in one of the lower rooms, near the doorway to the old gunners' lodgings, a short misty figure. At first I thought it was simply a shadow and was about to walk past, but then it shifted slightly and nearly made me jump out of my skin. I grabbed pencil and paper and asked him his name and why he was still here. Unfortunately there is no possibility of identifying who he was, or is.

"... They said the conditions were good. They were bad," he moaned. "I beg and plead with thee lady, help me from this place! Misery must be my name, yet I was not christened with such a name. My name is Hal, after the king who had this place of misery built. I was a gunner, in charge of six men at one time, yet never a sergeant. The cruelty, the way we fought and died. To live was a treasury they told us.

I haunt the castle from top to bottom. So many who have been here to view have no memory of us who dwelt within. I have plagued them, so many, but no more. I can continue to live again, not of misery, I hope."

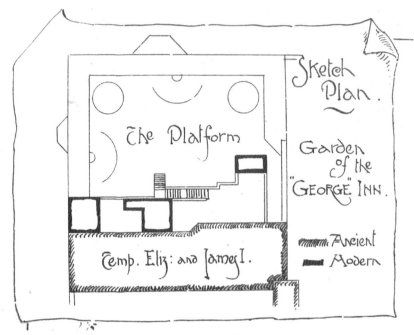

Plan of Yarmouth Castle.
Source Stone's Architectural Antiquities of the Isle of Wight

There was no sign of the ghost of Henry VIII haunting Yarmouth Castle; not that I expected to find him in a gun-fort rather than Appuldurcombe House, but there was always a possibility, perhaps even a hope, for I was running out of venues with royal connection. Nothing remotely royal found at Carisbrooke, Appuldurcombe House or the Royal Yacht Squadron, which was a bit of a 'long shot' anyway. I was beginning to wonder if I should look further afield to find a ghostly royal, perhaps even venture to London's royal palaces, if for no other reason than to prove it is possible for royals to become ghosts. Rogues, however, there was no problem finding those.

CHAPTER EIGHT

NEEDLES OLD BATTERY
LAST OF THE LAMP-WICK TRIMMERS

ATOP THE DIZZYING HEIGHTS over-looking the Needles rocks is the Needles Old Battery, one of Europe's most spectacular fortresses. It is haunted. A ghost in military uniform is often seen here, carrying his lantern around the gun battery buildings and through the tunnel to the old searchlight outpost high above the sea.

Since the successful sea battles of Admiral Nelson in which both the French and Spanish war fleets were mostly destroyed, England had felt secure from French or Spanish invasion. But during the 1850s France launched the world's first 'ironclad' battleship. Even if England built a thousand ships like HMS *Victory*, their cannonballs would just bounce off the iron sides of France's new fleet of battleships; but their broadside return would smash to splinters the timber-framed hulls of Queen Victoria's Royal Navy. While Britannia ruled the waves there seemed no need to strengthen coastal defences; but *La Gloire* and her ironclad sisters changed the situation. The British government ordered gun batteries to guard the two entrances to the Solent, and Portsmouth fired up furnaces to build iron ships of her own.

The Needles battery is a fearsome prospect, set atop sheer cliffs; together with the Hurst Castle fortification on the opposite shore these could trap an

The Needles Old Gun Battery

enemy ship entering the Needles passage. The first gun battery was manned in the summer of 1863 and by the following year was equipped with six big guns. Here were stationed one officer, two N.C.O.s and 21 men. The gun fort was next manned by Royal Garrison Artillery regiment gunners, when war was declared against Germany during the years of 1914-18; and in World War II the Isle of Wight Rifles were stationed here as the 530 Coast Regiment RA. But which one of them was doomed to remain at his post, as a ghost?

I first saw him in the long narrow tunnel that leads from the parade ground to the searchlight area. He walked toward me, though at first he did not speak. He stopped as dead as a dead man can, in his tracks, glaring at me; but I didn't feel comfortable in the eerie tunnel so I suggested he follow me onto the parade ground, where I took paper and pencil to record his particular views on war and peace, and wind.

"... First we build this place to defend us from the French, then the French are on our side. Shows how stupid war is," said he. "What a place to be stationed! Rather be at the front. Only a few of us, nothing to do when off-duty. No girls. Got to fighting among ourselves, me the worst. Defending England? Would rather be in the trenches.

I often had the job of filling the oil-lamps and trimming the wicks, no job for a soldier. I hated the tunnel, but at least it was out of the bloody wind. No man ever swore as much as me and always at the wind. North, west, south or east, all winds were like devils attacking me. The men laughed at me, all they thought of was beer, baccy and women. I only thought of dodging duty or getting out of the bloody wind. I neglected my duty, got told off. Swore I'd get even with the bugger. Never did. Some said I was mad. Maybe I was mad. They could have been right as when I died after the war, I found I was back here at the place I hated. Get me out of the blasted wind!

See another tunnel, better get to it for shelter. Do not know why I have been trapped. Was it the sin of stealing before I joined the army, or was it my fists that made me a ghost? Maybe I swore too much at the wind devils. Anyway, will get into the tunnel towards the light. See it is not a searchlight. Thank you, if you have helped me. So cold here, but maybe it will be warmer where I am going."

He did not provide his name, rank or number and so to which regiment or war he belonged - in fact who he was, or rather is - is anyone's guess; so too where next he might be stationed.

CHAPTER NINE
SHANKLIN CHINE
THE SPY WHO STAYED OUT IN THE COLD

S HANKLIN CHINE is one of the natural wonders of the Isle of Wight, a twisting Jurassic-Park like chasm wherein dinosaurs ought to graze. In fact this was the lair of a great sea serpent, a monster that helped to liberate Europe and carried the allied forces to victory in World War II.

Among Shanklin village's most famous peaceful residents was poet John Keats who came here to convalesce in the summer of 1819. He then was 24 years old, and while here noted: '… its wood and meadow and cliffs and clefts filled with trees and bushes and primroses which spread to the very verge of the sea.' Keats was here to escape smoky London, which aggravated his sore throat into what he feared would be the consumption to kill him. The poet of true love left the island later that year and travelled on to Rome where he died.

But in modern times Shanklin Chine is more famous as being the lair of a great sea monster that moved in during the reign of King George VI. For John Keats it would not be a thing of inspirational beauty, but to those allied commanders planning the D-Day invasions of Normandy, it was beautiful beyond words. October 1941, Lord Louis Mountbatten had received orders to report to the king and prime minister. Churchill was working on plans for an invasion of Europe, to push back the Nazi occupation of France. He asked Lord Louis to co-ordinate the effort: land, sea and air, and suggested he think of something Hitler wouldn't. To land an enormous assault force on the shores of fortress Europe with all those bunkers, guns and wire was difficult; but how to keep the force there, with tanks fuelled-up, was a real problem. Pumping fuel ashore from tankers anchored off the coast was doomed to failure from bad weather, enemy aircraft and U-boats.

During a modest wine and flame-throwing luncheon, arranged by the man from the Ministry of Petroleum Warfare, Lord Louis saw a solution to that problem. They watched spurt and flame and stared at scorched grass where before the hosts of daisies had sunned themselves. His lordship noticed the little ministry man's rubber tubing. 'Good God,' said he. 'That's it!'

Top Secret were the watchwords, but seriously scary were the thoughts occupying most islanders' minds on hearing mariners' tales of sea monsters in the coastal waters, for someone claimed to have seen the giant Channel Serpent rear huge coils out of the water and spew blood from its mouth.

51

Shanklin Chine, Isle of Wight

But few realised the monster was about to move into Shanklin Chine.*

June 1943, operations headquarters. The allied war leaders were gathered around the map. The meeting, code name *Rattle,* was attended by 11 air marshals, 20 generals and eight admirals; and among them the plans for liberating Europe were in deadlock. Lord Louis stood and rapped his baton on the table. 'Gentlemen we shall not land at the Pas de Calais. They know all about it anyway, damn the spies. We shall land in Normandy, and as for fuel,' Lord Louis pointed to the Isle of Wight, to Shanklin. 'Pluto will carry us to victory.'

'Pluto?' asked an air marshal.

'Goofy's dog?' asked an American general.

'Pluto,' said the man from the ministry. 'Pipe-line under-the-ocean. Or if you prefer, Pluto, ruler of the Underworld where Hitler will find a damned good roasting.'

Through Shanklin Chine pipeline Pluto, a reinforced pipeline, fuelled the allied advance into Europe. It pumped gasoline from the island right across the English Channel, all the way to Normandy, beneath the U-boats. The rest is history.

*Recommended reading on this fascinating subject is Adrian Searle's *PLUTO Pipe-Line Under the Ocean: the Definitive Story.* Shanklin Chine 1995.

Countless men and women lost their lives during that conflict, and their bravery will be remembered. But it was the small acts of treachery that cost the allies so much more. 'All is fair in love and war', is the saying but the ghost of Shanklin Chine will tell you otherwise. I found him near the remains of the pipeline. He too awaited a tunnel. But was it to be a tunnel up, or down to Pluto?

"... I have kept you waiting. I apologise. I was working on pipeline Pluto during the war. I was a spy, an Englishman who should have been shot as a traitor, but I was clever. I passed on information about the line to the enemy, and had years of luxurious living afterwards.

I died a sad man, as found a barrier prevented me from reaching the light which all are to reach. I have been here for so long, people coming and going, and making silly remarks about Pluto. That has irritated me. I have had to wait to confess and I realise I did harm, but not to the pipeline. That may be in my favour, or will it? My name is Norman, I am ashamed of all I did. How I communicated with the enemy, a traitor to my country.

Thank you for helping me, as a light shines ahead and I can continue my journey to the end of what appears to be a tunnel."

*   *   *

I did not expect to find a royal ghost in Shanklin Chine. No royal visits are listed here, though it is possible King Charles I, seeking an escape route, explored its steep sides and deep shadows during one of his rare excursions about the island. It is also likely that Queen Victoria came to see it during her long residence in Osborne House.

Neither was found haunting the chine. If there was any hope of finding a royal ghost, then the best possibility, so I thought, would be Osborne House where Victoria spent so many years, in happiness and in misery. If not there, then I would go looking in the old palaces at Greenwich, where the ghost of Queen Elizabeth is sometimes seen; and the Queen's House, nearby, where a ghostly royal was photographed on the Tulip staircase. Or the Tower of London, where the ghost of Queen Anne Boleyn is seen on Tower Green; or to Windsor Castle, traditional home of the royal family where so many kings and queens are laid to rest. Places with a host of ghosts, where I ought to find some royals among the rogues.

CHAPTER TEN
OSBORNE HOUSE
VICTORIA'S GHOSTS

ATOP the high ground on the eastern bank of the river Medina stands Osborne House wherein the empress Queen Victoria lived her last years and where she died. The empire since has shrunk, but many of its finest mementos can be found within these walls, though staff often complain that someone or some*thing* has since moved them to another place. At such times they whisper, 'It was the ghost!'

During the 1800s, young Queen Victoria and husband Albert sought a new home for their ever-growing family. Windsor Castle had no private gardens, Buckingham Palace had gardens but only attic-space for the children and the Royal Pavilion in Brighton was far too close to town. Victoria suggested a house on the Isle of Wight, a place not so very far from the capital, but an island where they both could walk without being followed or mobbed.

Albert inspected the site she had in mind; he examined its views and then decided it reminded him of Italy. Cowes, yes it would do, but the existing house had to go. Albert ordered it demolished and designed a sumptuous Italian villa. He and the family moved in to the new Marine Residence in September 1846, and apart from Highland excursions up to Balmoral and

Osborne House, East Cowes

54

state duties in London, the family spent as much time here as possible. On the 14th of December 1861, Albert fell ill and died in Windsor. Victoria was distraught with grief, so much so she retired from public life and instead sought seclusion at Osborne House. For the next 40 years until her own death in 1901 she refused to make any major changes to her dream home.

Even to this day, Prince Albert's portrait stands by her bed; his desk still next to hers in the sitting room; in fact Osborne House offers the visitor an experience of Victoriana frozen in time as to be found nowhere else in the world. Edward VII preserved the house as a monument to his mother, and closed the doors upon its ghosts.

Many people think of Queen Victoria as the grouchy old woman in black. Some thought of her as the Queen of Misery, though not those who really knew and loved her. A ghost waited by Victoria's desk in the royal apartments. She spoke a few words there to me; then wanted me to follow her out into the garden, all the way to a quiet part of the estate where Queen Victoria's bathing machine rests in state.

"... I was one of her ladies, the queen I mean", she politely added by way of explanation. "They often spoke ill of her, said she was a misery and so hard. Yet I found her charming and kindly. Of course we had to stand, never sit when waiting upon her. She was always polite and well mannered, as one would expect. One lady certainly said unkind things about her. I rebuked her many times which led to quite a nasty quarrel.

I shall continue my story to you outside. Go to her bathing machine if you can get there."

We left the house and made our way to the place where the bathing machine can be found at the bottom of the garden; and there she spoke again:

"The queen used this machine when she was young, and as an old lady she liked to visit it on the beach, occasionally. She stumbled once and complained of injuring her ankle. It wasn't really hurt at all but she held my arm until she reached her carriage. She liked to drive to the place where her children had played.

I roam between the bed she died on, and her desk. In the spring and summer I come out here where they have placed her bathing machine.

I loved her so much and wished to stay where she died. The other ladies, long gone, were so mean. One actually pulled my hair out of its pins. Fortunately Her Majesty never knew. I realise I now must go on to another realm and am pleased of this chance of speaking to you."

The haunted bathing machine, Osborne House

IN HER MAJESTY'S SECRET DISSERVICE

Within the palace gardens Victoria and Albert's secluded idyll was carefully maintained but beyond the garden walls their royal presence had entirely the opposite effect. In fields and meadows arose fabulous villas and fancy residences as the rich and famous chose an island home for their summer collection. The quiet secluded beaches and coves, secret night time haunts of smugglers and crablife, transformed into greens and promenades, paths and piers tipped with bandstands to create ensembles with crashing cymbals and crashing waves. The beautiful people came to the Isle of Wight to see and be seen and play upon the golden sands.

Britannia ruled the waves domestic and abroad, and above the staircase at Osborne House is a painting depicting the god Neptune presenting the crown of the seas and oceans to Britannia. In modern times few among those frequenting Cowes think of Neptune; though chances are the Romans built temples hereabouts in which to pay respect and give thanks for safe passage across the waves. Too few these days believe in such beings. Seas are seas, oceans are oceans and the winds just whistle and fill sails; the mastery of which mystery determines who might win a race at the regatta.

With Britannia mostly forgotten who now wears the crown? Lost it seems, but this at least had nothing to do with the naughty ghost of Osborne House.

"... Could not stand royalty," he snipped. "It appears unfair that every one must bow and scrape, as the saying goes, when the queen, the prince or the children passed. My name is Daniel; was in service in London in a lord's residence. When he died I was without work. Heard of a post going at the new house the prince had built on the Isle of Wight. I applied. After a long interview got the job as a footman. I lived in. The food was very good, the pay moderate, could save putting money by for my old age. Did not care for female company, had enough of them with so many female servants here.

I used to move objects around, especially on the queen's desk. Moving them to another part of the room causing time being wasted looking for something. Enjoyed muddling papers, a footman had this opportunity. I hid one paper of great importance, causing a minor skirmish; removed another document dealing with affairs of state, getting one of her ladies into trouble. It was my way of getting my own back, having to keep bowing and foolish-looking clothing.

Have still been moving things when I feel strong enough, but ghosts are not that strong all the time. Who are you lady who hears me and sends me on? Am not sure I want to go. I will, to be out of her way. Thank you."

There was neither sight nor sound of Queen Victoria at Osborne House, but I left the building wondering at the footman's wish to be "out of *her* way". To whom was he referring? But if Victoria was not to be found haunting her favourite home, then maybe she is not a ghost; or maybe it *is* true that royals do not become ghosts. Perhaps by virtue of their greater responsibilities in life, their after-death experience is different.

In order to find out for certain whether noble blood is truly a preventative against becoming a ghost - that royalty *is* immune from common haunting - I would go and look in some famous royal palaces and castles. There was only one place with a royal connection left on the island, and not a strong link at that, but first I was going to search for a royal ghost or two, to prove it is possible to become a ghostly royal.

I would begin my search in the world's most haunted castle, where two royals are believed to be ghosts: Princess Cecily's young brothers, the Princes in the Tower.

57

CHAPTER ELEVEN

TOWER OF LONDON

O NE of history's great unsolved mysteries is the disappearance of the two younger brothers of Princess Cecily, from the Tower of London. Their uncle, the Duke of Gloucester, was later suspected of ordering the assassination of 12-year-old Edward and his brother Richard, aged eight; leaving the duke as sole heir to his late brother's throne. The boys had been taken into uncle Richard's care following the death of their father, King Edward IV; and accommodated in the Garden Tower (since renamed the Bloody Tower as a result of this incident) to await Edward's coronation, as it was customary then for the monarch to spend coronation eve in the Tower of London, which was the principal royal palace.

Having placed the princes in the Garden Tower, Richard dismissed their attendant guardians. Lord Hastings, chamberlain to young Edward, was decapitated with a pole-axe on a log on nearby Tower Green; and then later the boys were found dead in their beds. At the time, uncle Richard was not suspected, but after his death suspicious minds claimed the duke had sent Sir James Tyrrel in to kill the children; and so this dark deed was described.

Some suggested it happened at midnight: Tyrrel, his groom Dighton and a murderous jailer named Miles Forest, entered the rooms where the boys were sleeping. They smothered one with a pillow and then cut the other's throat, and when done Tyrrel went in to make certain the children were dead. The bodies were hastily buried outside the Garden Tower but fearing their ghosts would come back to haunt him Richard ordered a priest to dig up the bodies and give them a proper Christian burial.

Gloucester's reign as King Richard III lasted merely two years. By the summer of 1485 he lay dead on Bosworth battlefield, in the last conflict of the Wars of the Roses. Dighton and Forest were arrested and begged for their lives from the new king, Henry Tudor, who offered them a deal of leniency if they found and returned the bodies. Unfortunately they discovered only that the old priest was dead and had taken to his grave the secret new location of where he had buried the princes. The two murderers searched the little graveyard in the chapel of Saint Peter ad Vincula, then elsewhere in and around the Tower grounds but the remains could not be found. Then someone claimed the murder had never happened. A man named Perkin Warbeck toured European courts claiming to be Prince Richard, younger of the two boys, grown to manhood. Henry was furious. He ordered every plan

Murder of the Princes in the Tower

of the fortress and much extra hole digging in search of the bodies, to prove Perkin was a fraud; but excavations found no bones matching the princes. Perkin asserted his right to the throne and raised an army to help him claim it.

Henry sent an army against him. Perkin was defeated and captured, and then brought as prisoner to the Tower of London where for two years his plans to escape were accompanied by the sound of Yeomen digging and swearing. He tried escape, he failed and he died; and on went the digging for even after his execution some people wondered whether Perkin truly was the man he claimed to be.

In 1674 during the reign of Charles II, labourers removing a staircase in the White Tower found a wooden chest buried three metres deep under rubble. When opened, inside were found bits and pieces of small human bones that could only be the remains of children. Examination revealed the bones to be the remains of two boys, almost the right age as the missing princes, and the right period. But were they really Edward and Richard? King Charles believed they were, and ordered that the skeletons be taken to Westminster

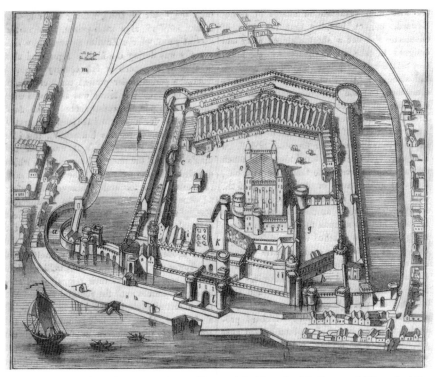

Tower of London plan. Beauchamp Tower 'c'. Chapel of St Peter ad Vincula 'd'.
White Tower 'e'. Bloody Tower 'k'. Traitors' Gate 'l'

Abbey, placed in a marble urn and given royal honours.

A ghost confirmed the king's conclusion, that the remains were those of the missing princes. It was during my springtime visit to the Tower that I found him in a doorway of the White Tower. He literally jumped out at me; and then followed, too close for comfort. But when he spoke his confession seemed as mysterious as the crime he claimed was his.

"... I committed a deed that in the golden days of Elizabeth or Henry I would have entered through Traitors' Gate and gone to the block," he said, excitedly. "I was with three other fellows when we found the chest. Upon opening, it was the remains of the famous Princes of the Tower. Some said no, but I know. I took three small bones, two fingers and a piece of small backbone to keep, to pass on to my children. The princes were taken away for a Christian internment.

Was I a thief who had to have these relics? I confess I did not know why. Perchance I was made to do this as it was when I died I went through a passage to be shown other lives I had lived, one being the fellow who smothered the princes. I had to return and haunt around here. You, a woman from nowhere, release me. My gratitude."

Without a name it is impossible to confirm if the ghost was Dighton or Forest; and his confession neither confirms nor refutes the involvement of Richard III, or even whether someone else gave the order. Nor does his confession of stealing bones as keepsakes verify his involvement, for the skeletons are far from complete. Many pieces are still missing including a skull, and who knows where that has ended up? But he did believe that the bodies were those of the two boy princes.

This ghost's presence in the Tower is especially interesting, because he claimed to have returned as a ghost from a *later* life that was connected with a previous life incident. He also spoke of other lives he had 'been shown'. This is not a reference I encounter often but it has curious implications: not the least of which is that someone else was doing the showing. Could it be that his desire to find the bodies of those children was so genuinely driven by remorse, the need for atonement and so foiled by failure, that he was permitted – or made - to return, to live again in order to find them, to put things right? Perhaps he accepted it was his responsibility not just to find the children's bodies but to confirm their identity, and then serve his punishment. It is one possible explanation for the connection between the lifetimes.

THE BISHOP'S HEAD

There were, and doubtless still are, lots of ghosts in the Tower of London but I did not find the two royal princes, even though they are said to haunt the Bloody Tower because of this incident. I did, however, encounter their murderer, and that is perhaps the better outcome. Those children suffered enough, without the additional torment of being eternally bound to this cold hard fortress. Others were not so lucky; and some of these came to talk as I explored the Tower in search of a royal ghost. One of whom spoke soon after I entered St Thomas's tower above Traitors' Gate; a man whose misfortune it was to live during the reign of a rogue royal, and had the courage to defy him.

The first official prisoner in the Tower of London was Ranulf Flambard, Bishop of Durham, imprisoned in the year 1100, on charges of extortion.

Surprisingly he managed to escape when the guards were drunk at his table, using a rope smuggled in to him. The next famous escape attempt ended in tragedy when in the year 1244 Welsh Prince Gruffyd ap Llewelyn, perhaps aware of Flambard's success, knotted together his shredded bed sheets and lowered himself down the wall. Sadly, the sheets parted and Gruffyd plunged headfirst to a bloody death below.

Other notable early prisoners included the King of France, John the Good imprisoned with his son in the year 1358. In 1415 following the battle of

Traitors' Gate

62

Agincourt Charles, Duke of Orleans, commenced a 25 year stay in the Tower on the orders of King Henry V; but since this fortress was also the royal residence, life here within these walls was not so bad. During the 1500s when King Henry VIII turned this fortress into his arsenal, mint and state prison, then conditions were much less favourable. A prisoner's journey into hell began at its mouth: Traitors' Gate, the main river entrance to the Tower complex; and their exit would be via discreet beheading on Tower Green or public mutilation outside the fortress walls, on Tower Hill.

Yeoman warders and Tower residents have often seen a ghost in old-fashioned clerical costume, especially in the rooms above Traitors' Gate, St Thomas's Tower; and for this reason assumed him to be the lost spirit of Thomas Becket who resided here when it was a royal palace and not state prison. However, the ghost was not Becket. He was a gentle old soul whose continued presence in the Tower of London was something of a surprise, if not altogether a mystery. It is understandable he could be mistaken for Canterbury's famous martyr for he was dressed as a churchman, but he lived in the Tudor times of Henry VIII, not Henry II.

I felt this ghost's cool presence around me as soon as I entered the rooms of Saint Thomas's Tower, yet he did not immediately speak. He drifted beside me, a misty figure in old-fashioned clergyman costume but it was only when eventually I decided to sit and rest and asked him who he was, that he chose to speak. His voice was soft and kindly as I took out my notepad and wrote as dictation what he had to say.

"... Methinks I am the most fortunate of wraiths. I wander o'er the Tower, from oldest to newest building. One unhappy time I the bishop had with endeavouring to make His Majesty heed me, yet he heeded me not, hence I was brought forthwith to the Tower, suffering great hardship.

Alas my life ended abruptly as I was led out to a cheering crowd. My name was one John Fisher, yet what is a name? The only thing a man has given him. Work for anything in life is the rule. To allow the monarch to have his way would have sinned against mine own name. Yet have his way he did, methinks. Thou art a gifted soul to help an old man on."

Bishop John Fisher

The ghost provided both first and surname, and with this information it was possible to identify him as John Fisher, former Bishop of Rochester and one of the Reformation's early victims. He not only bravely rejected the validity of King Henry VIII's divorce from his first wife Catherine of Aragon, he also refused to accept Henry's plan of assuming the title of Supreme Head of the Church. Bishop Fisher was an elderly man of 74 years when, in the year 1534, Henry ordered his arrest and imprisonment in the Tower. Fisher was harshly treated and denied warm clothes and decent food. When the pope heard of this ill-treatment he promoted him to the rank of cardinal and sent the red hat of office.

Henry was angered. 'The pope might send him the hat, but Fisher will have no head to put it on,' he fumed. Fisher was charged with treason despite his declaration that even if the hat was left on the ground at his feet he would not pick it up. Henry was not convinced. 17th of June 1535 Fisher was sentenced to a traitor's death. The court pronounced the decision: 'Your sentence is that you be led back to prison; laid upon a hurdle, and so drawn to the place of execution; there to be hanged, to be cut down alive, your privy members cut off and cast into the fire, and your bowels burnt before your eyes, your head smitten off, your body quartered and divided at the king's will. God have mercy on your soul. Amen...'

The place of execution was outside the Tower walls, on Tower Hill where traitors were put to death in front of the crowd. Fisher's death is documented: on the morning of his execution he was at last granted a fur cape so the crowd would not mistake his shivers of cold for fear. As the guards carried his frail body to the scaffold the ex-bishop held up his Latin Bible to the people come to see his death and said, 'O Lord! This is the last time that ever I shall open this book!' While the executioner made ready, Fisher prayed for the king and for the country's happiness then knelt on the straw before the block; and as the crowd pressed closer to watch he cried 'Let some comfortable place now chance unto me, whereby I, Thy poor servant, may glorify Thee in this my last hour.'

As a sign of respect Henry let him off the privy-burning and granted him a swift death by axe blow, but the guards left his naked corpse on the scaffold until evening, when his body was hoist upon a pair of halberds and carried back inside the Tower and buried in the chapel of Saint Peter ad Vincula. His head was par-boiled and stuck on a pole on London Bridge.

It is fortunate for the ghostly bishop, and for those many others who suffered the same fate, that an axe may sever flesh but not the spirit.

Tower Green, the scaffold site and Beauchamp Tower

THE GHOSTS OF TOWER GREEN

Tower Green is a rectangle of lawn and stone that accommodates the former site of special execution. Closely adjacent to the old site of the block is the Beauchamp Tower, and just a few paces on is the Chapel of Saint Peter ad Vincula (Latin: *In Chains*) whose graveyard was described as the 'saddest place on earth'. On this old site of execution beside the chapel were put to death five women; among them was Anne Boleyn, by sword in 1536. Her mutilated body was left in an elm arrow chest. Another was Margaret, Countess of Salisbury in 1541; niece of Yorkist Edward IV, her very existence earned King Henry VIII's suspicious displeasure. The countess was hacked at with several swipes before the axe-man landed a killer blow. Here also was executed in 1542 Jane, Viscountess Rochford.

For many years, longer than anyone can remember, yeoman warders and others working in nearby Beauchamp Tower have heard ghostly sobbing. Some have seen a misty shape at the windows that overlook the site of the executioner's block. Most think it is the ghost of young Lord Guildford Dudley whose family's political aspiration ended in execution, and that of a queen of England: his bride Jane.

For when Henry VIII died in January 1547 his only son and heir Edward VI was in favour of the new Anglican faith, but his health was so weak those close to him guessed he would not see his sixteenth birthday. Half-sister Mary, next in line of succession, was certain to put a stop to the Reformation if ever she came to power. Edward was made aware of this probability and for this reason, as he lay dying he agreed to an idea proposed by Dudley, Duke of Northumberland, to nominate Lady Jane Grey - Edward's first cousin, once removed - to succeed him in place of Mary. Jane was the granddaughter of Henry's sister, Mary. When questioned about the amazingly fortuitous timing of the recent marriage between Lady Jane and his own 17-year-old son Lord Guildford, the duke clasped his hand to his heart, looked innocent and spoke of piety, love and the good Protestant cause.

But others suspected there was more to the arrangement, such as how Northumberland would be father-in-law to the Queen of England and thus prime mover behind the scenes; and some wondered whether his end-game might even be murderous. Sixteen-year-old Jane had fainted when told the news she was to be Queen. Despite her objections, and the wily duke's reassurances this was God's will, unhappily Jane agreed to attend the Tower two days after Edward's death, on 6th July 1553, to receive the keys to this fortress as royal ceremony required; but it was the duke who grabbed them before passing them on to nervous Jane. Her reign as Queen of England lasted only nine days. The Duke of Northumberland's forces would not carry out his orders to arrest Mary who, when informed of brother Edward's death, claimed the crown; and thousands supported her. Northumberland's forces turned against him and by 20th of July the duke himself proclaimed Mary to be the true Queen of England. She ordered his arrest and his family taken to and imprisoned in the Tower of London. Jane's father, Henry Grey the Duke of Suffolk, likewise proclaimed Mary to be the rightful queen and told his daughter to remove the robes of state. She did so contentedly then asked him to take her home but he, to prove loyalty to Mary, refused. Northumberland, ex-queen Jane and Guildford were tried for high treason and brought through Traitors' Gate under sentence of death. The duke was imprisoned in the Bloody Tower and his sons, Lord Guildford among them, were confined in the Beauchamp Tower. Jane was given the opportunity to convert to Catholicism and by so doing save her life, but she refused to renounce her Protestant faith.

Before death the duke announced that he had always been at heart a good Catholic and never really wanted Protestantism, but still no one stopped the execution. His son Dudley, when it came to his turn, wept as he was led across Tower Green past the scaffold made ready for Jane. Like his father, he was put to death on Tower Hill; his headless corpse brought back in a handcart. Then it was time for the death of Jane Dudley. Guards led her to the scaffold on Tower Green, made ready beside the chapel. Witnesses to the event recall that when blindfold upon the scaffold the executioner had said, 'Kneel in the straw madam.'

'You will not take it off before I lay me down?' she asked.

Execution of Lady Jane

'No, madam,' said the executioner.

'Where is the block?' In her blindness Jane could not feel the block and no one could move to help her, such was the effect of the pitiful sight; even the axe-man held his breath. 'What shall I do?' A spectator stumbled forward and guided her fingers to feel the curve in the wood. 'Lord, into Thy hands I commend my spirit...' were the last words of Lady Jane.

Since Tudor times yeoman warders have seen the ghostly figure of a woman waft across Tower Green to the old site of execution. Her progress accompanied by the sound of weeping in nearby Beauchamp Tower. Some people say this is the ghost of Anne Boleyn, others believe it is the mutilated Countess of Salisbury.

On a spring afternoon when the grass is strewn with drifting cherry blossom from the trees Tower Green is a surprisingly pleasant place to sit and rest. Perhaps it is the presence of such softness amid the high battlements and shadowy valleys of grey stone, a softness that soothes the sense of trepidation that accompanies a psychic's visit to the Tower of London. For in some places the stone drips with condensation as if those souls who suffered here wept so hard, so often, their distress was absorbed into the stone, passed from one to another, and here it has remained. There are yeoman warders who claim the ghost of Tower Green is Lady Jane, and the weeping is that of her young husband Lord Guildford Dudley. And they were correct.

They came to speak to me as I waited beside the site of the block. I saw two misty shapes appear by the Beauchamp Tower. They were together but first to speak was Dudley, then Jane.

"... Help me. Help me. Help me! Am innocent of all treason. I wish to live in this fair land, to be with Jane. I plead, help me. Help me! I am innocent. I was so young, so was she. Help me, I plead and beseech thee. Thou hast ears and send me forth. I thank thee for this gracious act. Am Dudley."

Then immediately after.

"... Oh my beloved! I heard him scream. I would not when the time of myself came. Oh that I have had to linger so long around the block. My neck severed soon after my beloved. That the greed of the family should push me to reign over this country for so short a time.

I tarried too long before entering the passage to the next world, seeking my beloved. That thou shouldst find me is but a miracle. Religion, politics and greed, the fault of so many. Methinks I may be released from this prison of hate."

And then they were gone. Lady Jane was the first ghostly royal to be found; though Queen Mary's supporters might say that her presence here did not disprove the theory that royals cannot become ghosts, because she was not the genuine Queen of England. But royal ghost she was, and Jane had a good explanation for why that had happened. She believed that her continued presence in the Tower of London was because she had "... tarried too long before entering the passage to the next world."

Reference to lights or passage is often mentioned by ghosts, and by people who have provided witness accounts of their near-death experiences. In modern times science suggests this is just a hallucination caused by the brain's final transmission before its death. So, this means either we as a species are pre-programmed with this extraordinary 'exit scenario' vision; or what Jane and these other people tell us, *is* true.

The truth is we each will find out, sooner or later. But my opinion is Lady Jane is right; and she discovered that this passage opens shortly after the moment of death but is not permanently open. If the individual does not go through for whatever reason, perhaps to stick around and look for someone they love; or goes through and turns back, he or she will find the passage closed and they are stuck. This is to become earthbound: the physical body is in no state to be reanimated nor is there access to what Jane called 'the next world'. There are many theories to explain a ghost but this is the simplest, the oldest, and in my opinion the most accurate. There truly is a separable body, call it a soul or spirit if you like, that survives death. Ghosts are those of us who cannot get through the passage either by choice, accident or intention of those who wait beyond.

AXE OR SWORD MILADY?

Waiting patiently at the old block site was another ghost. I have often wondered what ghosts find to talk about during the long periods of their haunting; they must be aware of each other, as Samuel seemed to be. Had Jane been condemned to listen to Sam's glowing appreciation of his former trade and his pride in losing no sleep? No wonder Dudley wept.

"... It were me work, and good it were," said axe-man Sam. "Ne'er troubled me heart. Ain't got one, me wife said. Me name be Samuel, was one of the best at me work. Queens, dukes or just folk who angered his majesty went to the block. Some the sword had, that be for others to wield. I were for the axe. Many a purse I would receive for a quick blow. I were the best, ne'er a moment's slumber lost. Many thought me an unworthy soul and denied slumber. The best work for a real man, not a scented fool like some. Yet prisoner I be here, like so many. Methinks the time has come and go I will."

Contrary to popular opinion I do not think Anne Boleyn is among the ghosts of the Tower of London, for certainly some remain. It took several visits to help all these whose words I have related, and more, including those found outside on Tower Hill; as tuning-in to ghosts is extremely tiring. Somehow I feel sure Anne Boleyn would have spoken during those three days during which I was there. Unless of course, she wished to stay but that seems to me an unlikely choice.

And surely the priest found haunting the chapel of St Peter Ad Vincula would have known if she was a ghost of the Tower? That is, assuming he is speaking here of Queen Anne Boleyn.

"… I speak to thee outside, yet I the holy one in this chapel haunt here. Preached many a sermon and served the queen at her funeral by speaking the words that were placed before me in writing, not mine own. This grieveth me, as wished to give an oratory upon her goodness, not her badness. I hast had a guilty feeling ever since that fatal time and hast kept me here.

To preach of God maybe is wrong, yet to preach evil that wast not truth was more than wrong. Forgive me dear queen, your majestic bearing at the end is always before me. Mayhap canst join thee somewhere to showeth mine sorrow. Farewell to thee who pens mine words as I leave at last."

THE GHOST OF THE BLOODY TOWER

Of the world's most infamous buildings the Bloody Tower is probably the most famous, even though it was once sweetly known as the 'Garden Tower', and was V.I.P. accommodation. Some say it was here in 1478 George, Duke of Clarence, brother of Edward IV, drowned in a butt of malmsey wine. The guards found him dead with his head hanging over the side, though no one knows for certain if he actually drank himself to death rather than face public execution for plotting against the king, or was murdered.

He and a whole gang of ghosts are claimed to haunt the Bloody Tower. Many people assumed it to be haunted by the ghosts of the two murdered princes. Other ghosts believed to haunt this building are ex-residents Judge Jeffreys of the 'Bloody Assizes', imprisoned here in 1688, who died of drink and fright; and also Henry Percy the Earl of Northumberland who in 1585

The chapel of St Peter ad Vincula

committed suicide here. However, it is highly unlikely that so many ghosts haunt this tower; it would be far too crowded. Most likely the supernatural occurrences can be attributed to one ghost resident in the Bloody Tower, though probably from time to time the goodly roaming Bishop Fisher put in a ghostly guest appearance to cheer its long-suffering inmate who long ago was confined here, condemned as a rogue by two royals.

The Bloody Tower overlooks Traitors' Gate. It is a surprisingly small building for such a big reputation. Above the arch is a small room and a tight stone doorway leads into a narrow stone stairwell to the upper chamber, and on climbing these steps I could sense the many fingertips that have trailed the stone's cold hardness. The staircase leads up and then out to Ralegh's Walk, named in honour of probably the most famous resident of the Bloody Tower: the Elizabethan adventurer Sir Walter Ralegh. His fondness for one of Queen Elizabeth I's maids of honour, delightful Bess Throckmorton, resulted in imprisonment in 1592.

The couple married in nearby Saint Thomas's Tower, and son Carew was born within these fortress walls. Ralegh was eventually released but was then re-arrested on the orders of Elizabeth's successor King James who put him back, charged with treason. Ralegh was condemned to death but as he knelt on the straw before the block, preparing for departure, the king sent word that he had decided to commute the death sentence to life imprisonment, and so Ralegh returned to the Bloody Tower where he remained for the next 13 years. Crowds of people each day gathered along the riverbank to watch when he made his daily walk along the battlements; they waved and cheered. The Elizabethan world's celebrities came to visit him; among them, to King James' irritation, the queen and their son Charles, Prince of Wales. The prince loved hearing Sir Walter's tales of adventure, and was fascinated by his hen-house laboratory and his plans to write a best-selling book on the creation and history of the world.

But King James' bad temper festered. He appointed a new lieutenant to the Tower, Sir William Waad, with strict orders to make life less comfortable for Ralegh. Waad ordered Lady Ralegh, who chose to live with her husband in the Tower, to leave. Then, for no good reason whatsoever put Sir Walter in a damp dungeon, where he soon began to suffer.

His doctors appealed against such harsh treatment, the lieutenant was persuaded to relent and Ralegh did recover; and with his returning strength there appeared upon the horizon a plan of escape.

Ralegh appealed to the king, seeking release to guide an expedition to South America, and said if he did not find a mountain covered with gold and silver, up the Orinoco River, the commander could cut off his head there

The Bloody Tower

In 1671 Ralegh led an expedition along the Orinoco River

and then. The king agreed. In 1617 Ralegh set sail for South America. Sadly the expedition failed, Ralegh arrived back in England and tried to scoot to France but was arrested in Plymouth before he could and was brought back to the Tower. The king decided it was time for Ralegh's death.

On the execution scaffold the former adventurer refused to be blindfold. The headsman trembled so much he could not raise the axe. 'What dost thou fear?' asked Ralegh. 'Strike man strike!' When Sir Walter Ralegh's severed head was held up for display there was silence throughout the crowd. But King James was happy, for he was working on a book of his own about the history of the world.

The rooms of the Bloody Tower now are furnished as Ralegh would have known them, and it was in the upper chamber by the window that he waited.

At first I saw only a shadow and thought it merely a trick of the light, but the shadow moved and I could see more clearly a man dressed in Elizabethan doublet and hose. His face looked so gaunt, so drawn and miserable. I spoke softly and he came toward me.

"… Thou hast come. I have waited, why didst thou tarry so long, so long?

One majestic being did not forgive my marriage, yet love hath to lead one onward. My love stayed with this unworthy soul. I prithee send me to a place where no axe-man hath the head of such as I. It is hard to speak yet try I must. The axe was sharp.

My long voyage across oceans of desire hath ended, as another voyage is about to come to pass. Thanks be! Thanks be thou spied me by yonder window. So long a time. Walter is the name I was given, fare thee well helping many who roam here."

I can only speculate as to why some people become ghosts, or earthbound, while others do not. I am not so naïve as to believe that what these people tell me is all they have to say. Sir Walter Ralegh had led a colourful life, both light and dark, and some historians now suspect his deeds were not always for the good of the world; and not always in the best interests of the arts.

But he has served his time in the Tower of London, more than he ever dreamed possible.

So far I had found one royal, a goodly man of God, the last of the great Elizabethans and various rogues. While I was in the area, I thought to head down-river to Greenwich, to the site of an old Tudor palace where the ghost of Queen Elizabeth I is sometimes seen.

CHAPTER TWELVE
GREENWICH GHOSTS
PLACENTIA & THE QUEEN'S HOUSE

EASTWARD from the Tower of London, along the river Thames, are two famous historic royal buildings: the old Royal Naval College and the beautiful Queen's House. This area has known royal glory, for one of the greatest of all the Tudor palaces stood here: Placentia, a vast rambling red-brick riverside complex of courts, halls, chimneys and turrets. Within its walls and gardens Henry VII made love with Elizabeth of York and Henry VIII was born. In Placentia, Catherine of Aragon gave birth to Henry's daughter Mary; and here, on a giant bed, Anne Boleyn gave birth to Elizabeth and then, much to Henry's dismay, a stillborn son.

Placentia is now no more, though what stands in its place is equally magnificent: a vast palace of grey-white symmetry and tall Corinthian pillars in avenues of colonnades crowned, on the architect Christopher Wren's suggestion, with a fine pair of shapely domes. Today the new palace is part of the University of Greenwich; before this the Royal Navy used the building, and of this no doubt Henry VIII would be proud. This stretch of river was the home of his navy and here dressed in sailor's smock of cloth of gold, he inspected his war fleet; trolling around blowing his silver whistle.

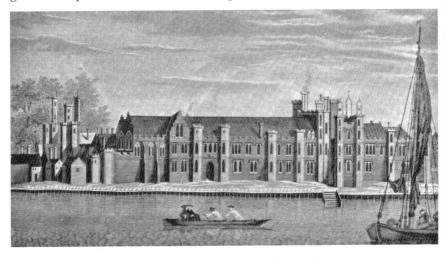

Palace of Placentia, Greenwich, London

76

The university building, Greenwich, London

However, it is difficult to picture Placentia's great past for the present building has mostly flattened that history. Much water has flowed on by since Greenwich's golden days when all was dazzling splendour, when Elizabeth of York travelled from here upriver for her coronation; a glittering flotilla among which was Henry Tudor's great red dragon spouting flames upon the water.

The ghost of the old Naval College has frightened people for the best part of 500 years, and perhaps she enjoyed the mix when the Tudor palace became prison, mission and biscuit factory during the civil war of the 1600s. Those who have seen the ghost describe Tudor costume and the haughty way in which she carries herself has led many to think this to be the ghost of Queen Elizabeth I whose favourite palace this was.

I saw her first by the eastern block of the building. It was evening and there were few people around. The ghost appeared through the wall and turned toward the river. I called to her as she drifted across the square and she stopped, and then looked round. Then she came toward me at a quick pace and next her voice was hissing in my ear.

"... For shame that I cleft to this exalted position," said she. "Mistress of the Queen's Robes. Woe unto any underling that doth not execute her duties to time, and well! Her most gracious Majesty had a temper that only I could quell. My voice was as sweet as honey when with the queen, yet hard like an iron bar and as sharp and deadly as a sword when giving orders to those under me. A serving wench swooning at my feet, her belly growing larger with bastard child, I kicked causing the unborn babe to be lost.

I regretted not. Hiding this deed from Her Majesty, yet not hidden from those who judge in heaven. That is why I tarry here clinging to my title, Mistress of the Robes. Yet thy presence pushes me away from here. Whither shall I go? I know not, neither am I merry over it, yet can tarry no longer."

The ghost of the university *was* Tudor but not the queen. It was her Mistress of the Robes, but without a name of course it is impossible to say for certain or even whether 'Her Majesty' referred to was Elizabeth I. But there was a ghost to be found in Greenwich whose identity was obvious, and she *was* once Queen of England.

THE QUEEN'S HOUSE

In 1966 a ghost was photographed on the elegant tulip staircase in the nearby Queen's House. Following a visit by Reverend Hardy and his wife they returned to their home, developed their holiday photos and were surprised to see a ghostly figure on the stairs. At the time the reverend had taken the picture he and his wife were there alone. Their photo was given to the Ghost Club who in turn gave it to Kodak for analysis. Tests suggested that no trickery was involved, and that what was there, *was* there.

The Ghost Club decided to investigate the staircase and for a whole night watched thermometers and cotton trails. Some members clicked away with cameras while others filmed the stairs, but by the following morning had produced nothing; only claims to have heard footsteps which were not their own.

There are many theories concerning the identity of the figure. Some suggest it is a ghostly monk who climbs the staircase, for long ago this was the site of a monastery. Others tell of a murderous crime of passion involving quarrelling lovers; others claim it is the distressed soul of a woman who dropped her baby down the stairwell. But the most popular theory is that it is the ghost of a Queen of England.

The foundations of the Queen's House were laid in the summer of 1617 for Anne of Denmark, wife of King James I. Anne chose an unusual site for the new mini-palace: it was built upon Placentia's old gatehouse that

78

straddled the busy road to Deptford where according to legend, in one wet moment Sir Walter Ralegh laid his cloak across a puddle for Queen Elizabeth I. The architect Inigo Jones designed plans for two blocks either side of the road and a first-floor bridge room across. The queen died in the spring of 1619 so work upon the building stopped until James gave it to son Charles, and Jones was recalled to complete the palace for daughter-in-law Henrietta Maria. Charles and Henrietta Maria spent happy times here with the family until catastrophe tore them apart.

In the summer of 1649 Parliament ordered all properties belonging to the ex-royals to be sold. Placentia became first a biscuit factory and then a prison. Who knows what kind of mess it was in when King Charles II returned here to the Greenwich palaces after the Restoration.

He decided to tear down old Placentia and build again, but for some reason the Queen's House was left mostly undefiled by the Puritans. It is said they appreciated its pure simplicity, albeit being Italian inspired and known as the 'House of Delight'. In the year 1662 Henrietta Maria returned to inspect the damage. She decided the little palace should be enlarged and beautiful bridges constructed. Then she left the country and went home to France, where she spent the last years of her life.

The Queen's House is now a museum of art, and at night its many rooms fall quiet to an air-conditioned hush. A welcome improvement, perhaps, for

The Queen's House, Greenwich, London

Greenwich's famous ghost, for it must have been frustrating during her long years of haunting, especially when the Greenwich site became a hospital and home for retired sailors. In her old palace the ghost would enviously have watched as countless salty souls drifted slowly out of consciousness and life, via dreams of the high seas.

The palace is a maze of panelled rooms now filled with paintings, and that spring day of my visit a tour party of French schoolchildren. I wondered if any were aware of the ghost as she followed me around, a shadow-figure seeking opportunity to speak. The children shrieked and talked so much I could barely hear their ghostly sister. Then, for a few moments in the galleried hall, there was enough quiet to hear and note a few of her words as she spoke of her regrets.

"...The English they hated me," she sighed, so softly. "Said I was extravagant and changed my mind too many times over important matters. I loved my husband, yet it appears I could have hastened his untimely and horrific death.

I died in my native land, France, yet am back here where I once lived as a queen who knew sorrow. So much my own doing. I regret much, regrets are too late. I can rest in peace now. You have a gift of releasing souls, I see this.

I bid you adieu madam."

Queen Henrietta Maria

Born 25th November 1609, Henrietta Maria was the daughter of French King Henry IV and Marie de Medici. Despite her intention to remain in England after the Restoration, ill-health due to bronchitis, brought on, so she believed, by the English weather was the reason she chose to leave the country in 1665. She died four years later, in Colombes in France, from an overdose of opiates prescribed by the royal physician.

The ghost of the Queen's House in Greenwich was a royal; no doubt about that, or her ancestral place at the heart of Europe's royal families.

So far I had found two queens of England, but no kings. My journey home would follow the escape route to the Isle of Wight used by Henrietta Maria's husband, Charles, which passes the world's most famous castle - Windsor - wherein he and so many other kings of England are buried.

CHAPTER THIRTEEN

WINDSOR CASTLE
ST GEORGE & THE DRAGON'S CURSE

Q UEEN HENRIETTA was safely out of the country when, in 1647, her husband King Charles escaped from London, heading for the Isle of Wight. He would have lost his way in that dark November night had he not recognised the lanterns on the battlements of Windsor Castle.

The castle stands on a lone high chalk outcrop above the river Thames. It is an elegant castle constructed of pale stone, at the heart of which is the round stone keep that divides the fortress into two wards: one houses the royal apartments and the other houses Saint George's Chapel which is haunted by a royal ghost.

Queen Elizabeth II and her royal family often stay here but there have been long periods in this castle's history when it has been left empty. Its massive walls, towers and halls have been costly to maintain and not all monarchs thought such expenditure worthwhile. Others have adored this castle. It was the favoured home of Queen Victoria until beloved Albert caught a fever here and died. George III loved the building; Charles II brought Baroque to

Windsor Castle, Berkshire

the old medieval ruin, in which his father's head was reunited with body. Henry VIII is buried here too, beside his beloved Jane Seymour; and many people believe Henry has not yet left the building. Various guards also claim a ghost is sometimes seen staring from the castle windows, a be-wigged figure that looks like His Majesty George III. Windsor Castle is also the home of the Garter and once upon a time, quite literally, the heart of Saint George.

There has been a fortress on this hill since the Conquest. Norman engineers saw this chalk outcrop, with its cliff-steep northern side, as an ideal defensive position to protect the western route along the river Thames into London. A mound 15 metres high was raised on the summit and two quadrangles surrounded by ramparts, ditches and a palisade to form a crown of wooden spikes upon the hill. Henry I built the first royal hall on the summit and held court here. In 1180 Henry II ordered half a mile of stone wall and construction of a huge stone keep atop the mound. Nine years later its defences were tested when the Archbishop of Rouen and the Bishop of Salisbury attacked Prince John sheltering behind his father's walls. John's guards panicked, opened up the gates and ran off into the forest where they were slaughtered. And among the many bad things for which King John is remembered, perhaps the worst was the imprisonment in Windsor and Corfe of the wife and son of his former friend William de Briouze. He ordered them chained in a dungeon with only a sheaf of wheat and a piece of raw bacon. When eventually the door was opened the King of England was unpleasantly delighted to see how the mother, before death, had gnawed at her own dead son's cheek where his head was bowed.

Such gruesome memory is mostly forgotten in the long history since, and those who visit Windsor Castle admire its vast solidity, its tall stately buildings, its right angles and tall arched windows. It is a huge updated medieval English castle complete with red-coated guards who stamp boots and shoulder arms.

On an overcast day Nick, who'd agreed to help with this ghost work, after the death of my husband, Walter, accompanied me. We climbed the slope of cobbled stone into the entrance, then on toward the crown of the Round Tower rising high above. The moat around the Conqueror's mound was lush green and bristling with daffodils. To the north of the mound is an elegant towered gateway known as the Norman Gate, through which we entered into the upper ward where the State Apartments are located, and a statue of King Charles II; and it was near this I noticed a misty shape. Nick was walking on but I pulled him back, and called to the misty figure. I could not tell if it was male or female, then as if startled it drifted towards us and soon was close beside me, and I took out pencil and paper to record his words.

"… Thank you for stopping to hear me. I would not wish to burden either of you. Was a famous architect, designed an extension on the castle that is so old. It looked natural, not just an addition. Was pleased, but not pleased with the workmen who took their time. They left their work for cheese and ale. This irked me. They would not work longer than ten hours and one half, six days a week. I allowed them the Sabbath.

It took so long to do this work. As I say, it irked me so much it took toll of my health, and when I died I was made to realise these men had feelings. My name does not really matter, prefer to keep it a secret, but my surname begins with an 'M', an important letter in the alphabet.

I can travel onward to heaven. I hope many will await me."

It wasn't much to work with, by which to identify him but he did give a clue. The names of architects who have worked on Windsor Castle are listed. The buildings in the upper ward were built for George IV who spent one million pounds creating his royal apartments, but his architect was named Wyattville. Before him, his father George III used an architect named Wyatt; so not him either. These two monarchs were the only ones responsible for recent construction work on the castle. The only other to have ordered building work was Charles II whose Comptroller of Works at Windsor was Sir Christopher Wren. It seemed there was no such architect involved whose name began with an 'M'.

However, further research revealed Wren was not appointed to his position at Windsor Castle until the year 1684, by which time most of the king's building projects were complete. Wren in fact made some plans but created nothing other than a new guardroom for the castle; but prior to his appointment Charles II commissioned a man named Hugh May to make major structural improvements to the old castle.

Charles had adopted Windsor as his summer residence and fancied, with some landscaping of the surrounding countryside, he could rival French King Louis XIV's palace project at Versailles. Charles wanted to restore Windsor's crumbling medieval fortress and give it a makeover into continental style. Although it was Wren's era, Charles appointed Hugh May as architect, and it is as a result of May's influence Baroque style was adopted into English architecture. In the autumn of 1675 May commenced work on the royal suite, now known as the State Apartments, removing the crumbling medieval buildings, and constructed a four-storey block with round-topped windows; before he died at the age of 66, on February 21st 1684.

After the deaths of Hugh May and Charles II, no more was added to the castle for many years. Queen Anne did not take up residence, she preferred to live in a small house down the hill; and following her death the castle fell into disrepair. For 100 years, rooks and pigeons made it their nest, local children their playground and various women had made homes in the old castle's towers. The castle remained so until George III, in the 1790s chose to make Windsor the family residence. His German predecessors had refused to spend any money on upgrading the fortress for royal habitation; but George jnr, interested in architecture and building, decided on a full reversal of the previous royal makeover. George did not like Charles II's continental touch and wanted to restore it to full Gothic glory; but because he had wasted so much money on other disastrous projects, he was able to do little more substantial than some refurbishment and hacking out a few windows and replacing them with good Gothic ones.

By 1804 he moved his family into Windsor Castle. Frustrated by how little he could achieve on the main castle building, George set about the old chapel of Saint George. He ordered his workmen to refurbish the noble home of the Knights of the Garter. Since there was no room left in Westminster Abbey for any more royal tombs, he prepared for himself and his heirs a new tomb-house beneath the chapel with space enough for 40 coffins.

King George's illness while living in the castle is well documented; but he was not the first to suffer, nor was he the last. Of all the castles in the British Isles, Windsor's story is among the most tragic. Of course during the long passage of time since a building first stood on Windsor hill, tragedy and ill-fortune are bound to occur. Notions such as curses can seem like coincidence combined in the mind of the superstitious; and the run of cruel fate visited upon all those who have lived in and loved this castle may be merely that: coincidence.

THE CURSE OF THE ROSES

Windsor Castle became the principal home of the English monarchy thanks to King Edward I, 'Longshanks'. He chose it as the safest place to house his mother, Eleanor, and his young children; a royal household inspired by grand events like the coronation feast during Easter 1275; and the tournament in the summer of 1278, when the finest knights in the country filled Windsor Park with their tents and banners and Crusader's tales from the Holy Land.

Grandson Edward III was the first king to be born on Windsor hill, and so styled himself 'Edward of Windsor'. Having imprisoned his mother, hanged her lover and punished the plotters who murdered his father, King Edward III ordered the first major rebuild and refurbishment of his favourite Norman fortress, and it was here that he came up with a cunning plan on how to

Artist's impression of Edward III's Windsor Castle

deflect the malevolent energies of his most dangerous subjects away from the royal person: War against the French. After early victories a great feast was arranged and all the king's knights gathered to make merry, during which festivities there dropped to the floor a garter, come adrift from the leg of lovely Lady Joan, Countess of Salisbury; and on sight of the accident there was much laughter and lewd comment among the knights. The king too noticed and in one swoop he picked up the garter, twirled it round his long fingers then slipped it up his own thigh. 'Sirs!' he roared to the astonished noblemen, women and clergy in the chamber, 'the time shall shortlie come when ye shall attribute much honour unto such a garter!' And the laughter stopped for everyone could see the king was serious.

In the summer of 1348 Edward announced the founding of his order of the highest chivalry - the Order of the Garter. All those who were members of the Order could expect tournaments, great feasts and the right to sit with the king at his new round table. The chapel was built to receive the Knights of the Garter who would take their place upon the Garter stalls, and thenceforth were to dedicate their lives to defending all that was noble, true and just.

But as time passed, Edward's brow furrowed deep as messengers brought bad news and more bad news of French victories against him. Worse was to follow, Edward grew feeble and his addled wits were the subject of much concern among the noble knights until his death in the summer of 1377.

Despite Edward III's romantic ideal of chivalry and noble errand, the years following the creation of his Order seemed anything but noble and just. To France's delight ill fortune descended upon the royal family and the whole English nation. Edward's eldest son the Black Prince died a nasty premature death and his ten-year-old grandson Richard was crowned king in 1377. When he was found dead in mysterious circumstances, cousin Henry accepted the crown and the misfortune got worse. For Henry IV's reign was plagued with plots and paranoia, while his subjects considered whether he was actually entitled to the throne when others still living had as good, if not better, claim to the title; and when he died in agony from seriously nasty pustulation of the skin, even they wondered if it was God's judgement on the wicked king's usurpation.

*   *   *

The lower ward of Windsor Castle slopes gently westward. Beside the famous chapel of St George is the Albert Memorial chapel wherein are the remains of Victoria's beloved husband Albert, who died here in the winter of 1861, aged only in his early forties. Directly opposite are the celebrated lodgings of the Military Knights of Windsor. It was there I found another Windsor ghost.

He only told me his first name, and of this he was not proud; so it is impossible to identify him. Castle guards and knights have often seen his ghostly form drifting across the ward, or heard muttered complaint as each sunrise leads inevitably to sunset. Time passes, guards change but he was doomed to wait for ever. Or so it seemed. He could not make the clock go backwards, but it was enough for him that it stopped, at last.

"… A villain in reality, but a gentleman to the world," said he. "I was a military knight of Windsor, and proud of belonging. To serve as I did was everything that one's heart couldst desire. The name my sire bestowed upon me was the most common of names, John. Often I wished I had been named something more appropriate to a man of my upstanding.

I cheated at games, whether on the table or in the field of sport, cheated my fellow men. Should one breakest a rule, was the first to report this to a superior. I wouldst that the clock of time couldst be put back, to live again. The great god of time doest not hold back the hours or the days. They passeth quickly. Have roamed the grounds of the castle for years, so long years, but can march onwards as a knight should."

And then he was gone. Who he was and to what era he belonged I do not know. By his language he had been a ghost of Windsor Castle for some centuries at least; though I doubt he had the honour of seeing the heart of Saint George, even if he had deserved to do so.

*   *   *

The heart arrived during the reign of Henry V, who had rediscovered the value of re-directing his subjects' bloodlust against their neighbours and again declared war on the French; and during celebrations over the victory at Agincourt in 1415 the heart of Saint George came to Windsor Castle.

Someone claimed to have found it and a few of his fingers too. The relics were high treasure indeed and on ceremonial occasion the priests brought them out to the altar whereupon they were unwrapped so the king and his knights could kiss them. Sadly, elation was halted for the Knights of the Garter, and in Windsor the townsfolk wept when Henry V died in 1422; the more so because he was about to be crowned King of France. He was only 35 years old, and everyone wondered how fate could be that cruel as to take him so early and on the eve of such triumph.

But son Henry VI was born in Windsor Castle, and so the knights consoled themselves that being Henry's seed, the boy must be a warrior. The noble knights cursed the French for rallying against them, and turned to their new young king to grasp the sword and lead them to victory. But no, the king preferred to study and to pray alone in his quarters. When he came out of his room it was no good talking of battle plans, he was far too busy wandering along the riverbank at the bottom of the hill, pacing, counting and pointing. All the king could talk about was how he wanted to build a school for boys where they would pray and study religion.

The military knights of the castle were downright frustrated when every morning Henry could be seen by the riverbank humming his favourite psalms, skipping among the workmen clasping hands saying, 'Yes, oh yes, it shall be lovely. Praise the Lord everybody, I command it!' And every night the knights stomped the castle ramparts clanging gauntlet against temple while the French took back all that fierce Henry senior had gained.

Some say it was the dungeon master who suggested the king needed a queen; and the court jester that she should be chosen from France. So word was sent, and in due course a ship set sail; but as it steered from the French harbour out into the Channel, at least a dozen sniggering Frenchmen were seen on the quay raising two fingers in the direction of England.

Within days of their marriage it became obvious that the queen felt more at ease than Henry among the knights and tough soldiers, but even these soon learned to avoid upsetting Her Majesty on days when she spat and looked fierce; which were most days. Then one summer's morning in the year 1453 Henry staggered about the castle in a strange way, then finally seized up completely in a catatonic state from which no one could rouse him, not even the close presence of cousin Richard, the Duke of York, who fancied his claim to the throne was greater than Henry's. It was agreed York would assume regency until the king recovered.

Even the veteran knights who had experienced many strange things in foreign lands were astonished when the queen announced she was pregnant. Some thought it might have been that experience which had turned sweet Henry's brain, for it seemed he did not relish the task, not even for England and Saint George. But the queen glowed; the king lay completely senseless, and the clergy, as always, prayed for his soul.

And their prayers were answered the following year, at the big Christmas celebration. For, after nearly 17 months of senselessness, the king sat upright in bed, opened his eyes, blinked, yawned then said he felt so much better.

Cousin Richard peered into Henry's eyes to make sure. The king saw the queen, saw her satisfied expression and asked what was wrong with her.

'Majesty,' whispered the priest, 'the queen has given birth to a son.'

But no one, not even the priest had the heart to explain how it happened and risk another seizure.

'Husband, we have an heir,' said the queen.

Henry's jaw dropped and quivered, he stared wide-eyed in wonder. 'I declare it must be the son of the Holy Spirit,' said he.

And cousin Richard knew not whether to laugh or cry.

*   *   *

Saint George's Chapel, on the north side of the lower ward, is a long ornate building of double-layered arched window and buttress, whose overall effect has been described as fine as the wings of a dragonfly.

Through the door and into the interior every visitor falls to hush as it becomes apparent that these are no ordinary tombs and memorials; the elegant pillars and craftsmanship are of no ordinary chapel or shrine. To walk the aisles beneath the delicate veined, fanned ceilings is to wander through a history-book hall of fame. Amid the marble and stone lay the remains of kings and queens of England from as long ago as Edward IV and Henry VI.

Beside the tomb of Edward IV is the entrance to the choir wherein the Knights of the Garter have their ceremonial stalls. The choir is not as large as other places of worship but it certainly is spectacular: a mass of intricate

Saint George's Chapel, Windsor Castle

carving of light and dark wood, and black and white chequered marble floor; and above the stalls are the dark carved canopies topped by colourful crests and banners, swords, helmets and mantling of the Order which continues into modern times. In the centre of the chapel's choir floor is a black rectangular stone to mark the tombs of Henry VIII and Charles I, and beneath the altar is George III's royal vault in which rest his son George IV and William IV.

As I gazed around admiring the truly historic scene, I felt a coolness descend around me. I felt for my pencil and paper, there was a ghost nearby; but before I could settle I felt someone grab my hair and yank back my head so I was staring upward, in pain. Invisible hands forced my head to look around at the colourful banners, then just as suddenly let go of my head and released me. Then a voice hissed in my ear, and I grabbed my pencil.

"... I made you look up. Not so many folk do. They look at the tombs in the floor. You see the hatchments, or flags as some call them? Those of royalty. Does anyone stop to realise the work that goes into making one, or that did in days gone by? All made by hand. I made several, a man of skill, but was unhappy that royalty should be so privileged, with their money, castles, palaces, jewels and possessions, while peasants and common folk lived on a pittance, on widows' mite, practically.

I was paid for my work, it only paid for the essentials of life for a man with four children and a wife to support. My eyes gave me trouble, but had a new invention to help me, eyeglasses. Not meant to haunt the chapel, yet could not leave for a reason that escapes me. My name is Thomas, Tom Tom they called me. Can go to where there are no flags."

As with the military knight, simply having a first name of Thomas is no use in identifying him. He said he had access to a new invention, of eyeglasses; however, rare mention of these dates as far back as the AD 1300s but more widespread access to them was probably during the 1600s. It is likely they would have seemed like a new invention to him; but it cannot be used to confirm to which period he belongs. Sadly, the full identity of poor Tom the hatchment maker will never be known.

*   *   *

Following the birth of Henry's heir, England became too busy at war with itself to trouble the French, who from time to time were reported to raise their goblets to Queen Margaret, who brought the armies of Lancaster and York chasing and fighting across the fields of England, north and south; while everything in between was pillaged, burned, raped and despoiled, much to Henry's horror.

In 1460 the Duke of York was slaughtered, his place taken by son Edward whose military skills brought him early victories. So much so he agreed to be King of England, despite the fact that Henry continued to wear the crown and wife Margaret, in most people's opinion, the royal trousers. In a bizarre series of twists of alliances, enemies became friends, friends became enemies; as in turn Henry was captured by the Yorks then Edward by his former allies, until finally gentle Henry was captured again and placed in rooms in the Tower of London. A move which did not wholly upset him; for it gave him peace and quiet to study and pray, away from the battlefield and all that pushing and shoving and foul language.

The Yorks moved into Windsor. The new king, Edward IV, inspected the castle. The chapel of Saint George looked in a disgraceful state of disrepair, its walls crumbling and its roof about to fall in. His architects suggested demolition and Edward agreed; for now he could build something special, a monument to the House of York. But first there was the problem of the

From 'The Game of the Chesse' printed by William Caxton 1480

Lancasters: what finally to do with Henry and his heir Edward, and wife Margaret the she-dragon. In their final battle in a field near Tewkesbury, in 1471, the Lancastrian army, led by Margaret and Edward, was defeated. She and her son ran for their lives, but the boy was caught and then slaughtered by York's brother Richard, Duke of Gloucester. Within days someone entered Henry's room in the Tower of London and smashed a sword through his skull; and some people still say the same man committed both crimes.

Meanwhile back in Windsor, Edward strutted and stroked his parchment plans as he watched the workmen raise his splendid new building. 'Like a dragonfly's wing,' they said and the new sole King of England agreed. It was superb, a fitting home for the noble Knights of the Garter. After all the years of bloodshed and treachery, at last now there would be a fitting monument by which to remember the sacrifice of so much English blood. Edward thought of the years ahead: a new chapel of Saint George for a new era, the House of York in ascendance. He thought of how his two sons the princes would take their rightful place here, and in due course Prince Edward would be crowned King Edward V. But that was a long way off. Or so it seemed.

Unfortunately, Edward's rosy future on Windsor hill was cut short by pneumonia. As he lay dying the two boy princes listened at his bedside to their father's final words: 'Don't worry,' he croaked, 'uncle Richard will take care of you both...'

91

King Henry VIII completed the building of the chapel. His parents, Elizabeth of York and Henry Tudor, surviving heir of the House of Lancaster, brought to an end the Wars of the Roses. Henry also built a new front gate to Windsor Castle. Henry loved this castle; he decided it would be his and Jane Seymour's final resting bed. But resting he is not. Many guards and castle staff say he haunts here. And so he did.

I found him in Saint George's Chapel, there tormented by Tom Tom whose bad luck at finding himself a ghost did at least provide him with an unexpected opportunity to discuss the merits of socialism and privilege with one of history's greatest, but now helpless, abusers.

> "… It has been told that I, the most spoken word of kings, would repenteth and haunt. Yea, this is correct. Those fools forgot me once, dead, forgotten. I requireth my way. Listened to those I wished to. Women, women! You who hast a gift from someone knoweth my story now. Ye can laugh at mine downfall. Gold, silver, jewels, not happiness. Praise be mine earthly remains were found by a means that were strong. I can be forgiven for many sins and go to the Creator.
>
> Thanks be to someone, or something. I sign this, Henry."

It is a mystery why some buildings attract more ill-fortune than others. Of course given great passages of time, good and bad things inevitably will occur; but some do seem to receive more than what might be considered fair share. Has Lady de Briouze's desperate agony at being imprisoned with her son in a cold damp cell, beset by ravenous hunger, caused such a chain of consequence? Before her last breath did she curse King John, his castle and all those to follow?

Or maybe she is not to blame; and to attribute to her the curse of the roses is merely to heap further punishment upon a lady who suffered more than she deserved. Indeed the curse may be older even than the castle walls; for archaeological teams have unearthed evidence that the Saxons, for some mysterious reason, built their main settlement further down-river, away from the hill.

It is impossible to say why, but tragedy does seem to strike the monarch and his or her family more in Windsor Castle than in any other royal residence. And lest we forget: it was on Windsor hill in 1648 that dour Cromwell's Puritan forces held their famous intense prayer meeting during which they called upon God to guide their actions over what to do with King Charles I.

In memory of Diana, Princess of Wales. 1961-1997

CHAPTER FOURTEEN

SWAINSTON MANOR
TIME-TRAVEL CHAPEL

TIME-SLIP ghosts are perhaps more of a mystery than others. Maybe these are, as T.C. Lethbridge reasoned, *atmospheric photographs*. It did not occur to me to try and ask the Niton 1920s group of women and children - discussed in chapter three, whom I saw looking for a lost cup - if they needed any help in their search; or to ask a monk as he walked past me at old Quarr Abbey if it really was Henry VIII's aunt Cecily in the coffin. I had assumed time-slips are simply moments captured in time, only replaying what has already happened but cannot be interacted with. Well, that is what I had assumed until two extraordinary encounters at Swainston Manor, a mile or so west of Carisbrooke Castle on the Isle of Wight, changed my mind. I describe them as ghostly encounters, but in truth it is difficult to tell who was the ghost. So I shall leave it to you to decide.

The first encounter happened during a warm mid-summer afternoon. An unlikely time to see a ghost you might think; but that day I was not ghost-hunting, just visiting, for the manor is one of the Isle of Wight's loveliest

Swainston Manor, Isle of Wight

93

locations. Walking along the drive toward the front door I saw a fair-haired woman to my left, sitting on a seat beneath a tree. I would not have thought anything of it, except she looked so out of place; like the 1920s group, as if from a fancy dress event but this time of another age. Instead of entering the hotel I walked up to the seat, expecting her to disappear but she didn't. So I sat beside her.

She did not seem at all like a photograph. As I stared, examining her outfit she in turn watched me with curious interest. She wore a long velvet skirt of mid blue and what looked like a matching collarless jacket and a blue velvet hat to match her dress, but this was an unusual shape: like a small upturned flower pot with a little knob on top. She had a pretty face, blue eyes, small features, nose and mouth. She wore a long thick gold chain around her neck, but I did not see any ornament attached to it. We sat together in silence for several long moments.

Then she moved, but she did not disappear. To my great surprise she reached down with her hand and touched my skirt, feeling the material and rubbing it between thumb and forefinger. I noticed on her right ring finger she wore a ring set with a large blue stone, and what looked like a gold ring with an emblem on her middle finger left hand, but I could not see what the emblem was. She seemed fascinated by the material.

"Polyester," I said, and then pointed to my T-shirt, "and this too."

She tilted her head in puzzlement. I touched her sleeve, "lovely velvet," I said brushing with my fingertips over its exquisite quality. She nodded, so I assumed she understood, and then she pointed at my bare legs; she seemed shocked at the short length of my skirt.

Perhaps it was that reaction; or the richness of velvet; or the thickness and quality of the gold chain and rings she wore that made me realise this was not a member of a charity theatrical event. 'This woman is real,' I thought. Next she was laughing at my open-toed canvas shoes.

"This is how most women dress these days!" I said; she was laughing and even as she did so I watched, amazed, as she vanished from the seat, fading before my eyes; and I was left alone on the seat.

Swainston Manor is now a beautiful hotel. It always has been beautiful for long ago this was the summer palace of the Bishops of Winchester. Although upgraded and renovated for the 21st century, the building still includes an old chapel dating back to medieval times. Many hundreds of years old, little has changed since a King of England came to stay on the Isle of Wight, in the year 1285. That king was Edward I, 'Longshanks'.

The king arrived at Swainston on 5th November 1285. At that time the island still was in the possession of the De Redvers family, descendants of

Swainston Manor chapel

good Lord Baldwin, who then lay undisturbed in the hallowed ground of Quarr Abbey. The redoubtable Isabella de Fortibus, the last of that family, lived in Carisbrooke Castle, and may have assumed, though not necessarily welcomed, the king's expectation of her hospitality at the castle.

Instead King Edward landed his royal party in the home of his Bishop of Winchester, and according to reports he turned rogue. It is said the king did everything he could to upset the bishop, who reluctantly signed away his palace and all its lands to keep His Majesty's favour.

I had forgotten about that extraordinary encounter with the ghost lady in the garden until several months later, when I was given an unusual mission. Ron Winter, the island historian and author, heard about this exchange. Excited, he asked if I would attempt to contact her again.

It seemed highly improbable to me, as so many months had passed but I agreed to try. Guessing she might be part of the king's entourage, from the description I gave him, Ron wanted me to ask her if the bishop who owned the palace, John di Pontiserra, was a native of the town of Sawbridgeworth in Hertfordshire, as his name translated implied. 'What chance?' I thought but accepted the challenge. Ron had in mind a particular day during which to make the attempt: 5th November, it would be the 708th anniversary of the king's visit. Ron wanted to know if the reason for that visit was to take possession of Newtown harbour which was part of the estate.

I sat alone on the manor garden seat; closed my eyes willing the time-slip to happen, but knowing such things do not happen to order. How to trigger it? I tried to picture the woman in my mind, as if to summon her, though I have never tried any such thing before. Ron watched from the porch. After half an hour or more of waiting I saw no sign of the lady in blue velvet.

Disappointed, we decided to try standing at the old palace doorway in the basement. We waited. Ten minutes, nothing; 15 minutes, nothing.

I was just about to give up when someone appeared in the old doorway, someone I recognised; but not at first, for she wore what seemed to be a soft light veil, rising upward. Her gown was dark, crimson-coloured velvet, and she wore a matching sleeveless long coat. She looked surprised to see me.

Something indefinable had changed, and I tried to think what it was: the time. It felt different; it felt like late afternoon, it wasn't dark.

"You have come back," she said. "You are the ghost from the future."

"Yes," I replied, for I could understand what she said, even though I didn't understand how. I felt I was being helped, somehow. And I felt comfortable being in her company, which was just as unexpected; in fact she felt like an old friend. "Are you here with the king?"

"Yes," said the ghost. "I attend to his needs when necessary."

"What do you mean?"

She just laughed at that, a high pretty laughter. She had a beautiful smile. She touched my velveteen skirt again. "You have velvet? Is it?"

"Not really," I replied. I touched the cloth of her gown; it was pure velvet, *real* velvet. On her feet she wore flat pointed red shoes, soft kid-leather I guessed. She asked me about the material of my skirt, and how many I had; and then told me she had 150 different outfits.

"What is your name?" I asked.

"Matilda." She asked my name, and I told her. She pointed at my feet, and asked how I kept my shoes on as there was no back to the heel. She seemed to want to talk about clothes but then stopped, and smiled thoughtfully. "Would you like to meet the king?"

"I should like to very much."

"I am sure he would like to meet you. Come to the chapel. We have been here two days and he is going into the chapel. And you will meet the bishop as well."

It was then I heard the sound of people inside the old chapel.

I don't know if Ron or I really expected this to work, but it did! There were people in the chapel, in medieval clothing, mostly men. I didn't see any other

Swainston Manor chapel interior

women. The lady stood in the chapel doorway as I came to walk in. "Now I shall take you to the king," she said leading me toward the front of the chapel to where two men stood near an altar; one dressed in a beautiful violet robe with fur trimmings down his surcoat, and lots of gold chains.

I didn't need to guess who he was, but the other I could only assume was the bishop, for he did not wear a bishop's mitre, he wore a skull cap. A cross-looking man, I thought. They weren't talking as we arrived. The chapel walls were plain stone; no glass in the window above the altar, just shutters at the side, and sconces on the walls on either side.

The lady curtsied to the king. "Sire, may I present a lady from the future?"

He looked at me, and I thought I must do something, so I curtsied too!

He put out his hand and raised me up. "I find this most interesting." There were two stools nearby, and he gestured to one. "Pray be seated." He sat on the other. He was not wearing a crown, he had mid-brown hair. "Where are you from?"

"The 1990s," I replied. "And I live on the Isle of Wight."

"How can you come back into our time?"

"I don't understand it, but I seem to have the gift for doing this." He was inspecting me, up and down. I felt shy under his close scrutiny; guessing he was trying to work out the numbers, years and possibilities. "May I ask a question?" He nodded his head. "Why have you come here?" It was the second question Ron had primed me with, to be asked if this worked.

"I have business to attend to, with the bishop," he replied. "He is a difficult man. This building we are in," he asked. "Is it still here in your time? And does it still belong to a bishop? Who does it belong to?"

"People run it as a hotel," I replied.

"What is 'a hotel'?"

"Have you come to Mass?" asked the cross-looking man, crossly.

"No," I replied.

"Why not?"

"I am not of your faith."

"A heretic," said the Bishop of Winchester.

"Can I ask you a question?"

"What is it?"

I asked him if he came from Sawbridgeworth.

"My father."

"Thank you," I said and then looked up. It was dark outside the window; and I was alone in the chapel. The bishop, the king; the gold altar cloth and candlesticks, all had vanished. The chapel returned to how you see it now.

King Edward acquired the summer palace, and then some years later he got the whole island from Lady Isabella. On her death-bed she signed it over to him. For certain he left that party weekend having witnessed a glimpse of the distant future. It was as much a time-slip for him as it was for me.

Who says time-travel is not possible?

It happened at Swainston Manor.

CONCLUSION

Ghosts come in all shapes and sizes, just like us, which is not a coincidence because they are us; well almost. But there do seem to be several kinds of ghost: the trapped individual whose body is dead, but cannot, as Lady Jane said, "pass through the tunnel of death" - whatever that *tunnel* might be. I call these souls earthbound, but not everyone is unhappy about this fate; some deliberately choose to remain so. Most, however, do not want to end up like this, and either missed the chance to pass through the tunnel, for whatever reason; or are made to wait. Of these latter it is fair to say that rogues do tend to stick around as ghosts, be they royals or not. For many, being a ghost seems to be a period of penance-in-place.

As for what comes next: the ghost responsible for finding the lost princes in the Tower of London implied there is more 'coming-and-going' to life and death, more than most people realise; so maybe we all do get our opportunity to be the royal and the rogue, for better or worse, for one life or another.

But maybe some people get to play those roles for longer than they expect. For what of those ghosts who replay as time-slips; are they just atmospheric photographs as T.C. Lethbridge suggests? My answer is that I do not know. Lady Worsley of Appuldurcombe House somehow has achieved both; but what of the royal court seen at Swainston Manor? Those courtiers responded to my presence in a real way. They were not images.

It is possible to speculate on the nature of time: we assume it to be moving ever forward. Our history books accrue dates and events as markers, but do some of us continue our unique role in the universe's epic drama; replaying life's curious and bitter sweet politics for the satisfaction of the great God of time? Britain has many marker carcasses such as old Quarr Abbey, the Swainston chapel and Appuldurcombe House, where what is visible is not all there is to be seen; and where secrets are not secret, to ghosts.

There is only one obvious conclusion to be made: each of us will find out the truth about ghosts for ourself, one day or another; but my advice to you is remember Lady Jane and Mary, Madam Butterfly. Mark their words and remember well, for when the passage opens for you do not hesitate, do not wait around or roam looking for something before you go.

Unless of course you want to become a ghost.

HISTORICAL NOTE
THE VELVET QUEEN

Bishop John Sawbridge, or 'di Pontiserra' as it was Latinised, of Swainston Manor probably knew the identity of the lady in velvet who came with King Edward 'Longshanks' to stay in his palace; and that she was not the king's wife, for he had been married since November 1254, when aged 14, to Eleanor of Castile, who died five years after his visit to Swainston. Nor was the lady Longshanks' second wife, Margaret of France, whom he married in 1299, when he was 60, and she was in her 20s.

There are no lists of King Edward I's mistresses. We can only assume he remained faithful to Eleanor and Margaret; or that his lovers trusted their secrets only to the ghosts of a future age. So who was the lady in velvet?

It is fair to guess that no commoner would be welcome in King Edward's intimate company; and that she was not, for she told me she possessed 150 gowns. If most were of the same quality as those I saw, then she would need to be very wealthy in her own right, and not in the gift of an empire-building married king. Only a few females with that name are listed for that period.

Mechthild of Magdeburg, born in 1207, would have been too old, though she had a reputation for mystical experiences. Matilda of Holstein, born in 1220, the Danish queen consort was also too elderly. Mechtilde of Hackeborn, who died in 1298 aged 57, was a saintly nun so probably not her. Matilda of Habsburg, born in 1253, Duchess consort of Bavaria was 32 when the king came to Swainston. Being already ten years into marriage with Louis II, Duke of Bavaria, probably ruled her out of Longshank's close affection; so too their daughter Mechtild of Nassau who was probably too distant and too young.

And historical dating must also rule out Lady Isabella of Mar, daughter of Domhnall I, the Earl of Mar, and Helen of Wales, the illegitimate daughter of Llewelyn ab Iorwerth, the Prince of Wales. Although her exact date of birth is unknown, though given by some sources as around 1275, (which would make her ten years old at the time of the king's visit to Swainston; and that the lady in velvet was not,) what *is* known is that the lovely and extremely wealthy Lady Isabella could speak Gaelic and English. Her father, one of the seven great 'guardians of Scotland', arranged for her marriage to Robert the Bruce, so gifting the family's considerable fortune to his cause. She was also known as 'Matilda'.

Lady Isabella died in 1296, soon after giving birth to their daughter.

It was in that year King Edward sent his army into Scotland.

APPENDIX
Discovery of Human Remains at Quarr Abbey.
January 1857

Agents in this locality follows their advertisement in this day's paper.

DISCOVERY OF HUMAN REMAINS AT QUARR ABBEY.

To the Editor of the Isle of Wight Observer.

Sir,—A week or two ago a vague report having got into circulation that several stone coffins had been discovered at Quarr Abbey by some labourers who are at present engaged in making a new road through the ruins, I was induced to pay a visit to the spot to ascertain, if possible, the truth of this statement. Upon going to the Abbey, I was at once directed to the place where the remains had been found. They were situated at a few yards to the south of the spot where the ancient Abbey Church once stood, and consisted of three small stone boxes or chests, each chest being about two feet in length and one foot wide. They were placed side by side, —two of them nearly close together, and the third a foot or two to the south. They all of them ranged in length from east to west. Upon removing the heavy stones, of which the lids were composed, I found three human skeletons in good state of preservation, all of which had been placed in these receptacles with evident care. The leg and arm bones were on either side, the ribs and small bones in the centre, and the skulls at the western end—the latter being in all three cases turned upside down, and all the loose teeth carefully put inside

To the Editor of the Isle of Wight Observer

Sir, - A week or two ago a vague report having got into circulation that several stone coffins had been discovered at Quarr Abbey by some labourers who are at present engaged in making a new road through the ruins, I was induced to pay a visit to the spot to ascertain, if possible the truth of this statement. Upon going to the Abbey, I was at once directed to the place where the remains had been found. They were situated at a few yards to the south of the spot where the ancient Abbey Church once stood, and consisted of three small stone boxes or chests, each chest being about two feet in length and one foot wide. They were placed side by side, - two of them nearly close together, and the third a foot or two to the south. They all of them ranged in length from east to west.

Upon removing the heavy stones, of which the lids were composed, I found three human skeletons in good state of preservation; all of which had been placed in these receptacles with evident care. The leg and arm bones were on either side, the ribs and small bones in the centre, and the skulls at the western end - the latter being in all three cases turned upside down, and all the loose teeth carefully put inside them. I at once saw that these remains had been removed at some time or other from the place of their original burial, and that they were of persons of distinction was beyond doubt, or such care would not have been bestowed upon them.

Upon a further investigation I found that the centre skeleton was that of an aged man; the other to the left was that of a female, evidently advanced in years, the teeth were much worn; and that on the right of a tall, fine man, about 40 years of age as near as I could judge by the appearance of the teeth,

&c. The next question was, where were they removed from, and who were they?

On looking into the history of this Abbey, according to Worsley, it appears that at its dissolution it was purchased by a Mr George Mills, a merchant of Southampton, when it was destroyed for the sake of its materials, "without respect to the sepulchres of the illustrious persons buried in its chapel." Those of consequence known to have been buried here are Baldwin de Redvers, or 'Rivers', Earl of Devon and Lord of the Isle of Wight, the founder of the Abbey; Adelina, his Countess; and a young son, Henry. This Baldwin died in 1155.

We afterwards find that William, the second son of Baldwin, who was surnamed de Vernon, from the place of his birth in Normandy, was buried here also. He was one of the four nobles who supported the silken canopy over Richard the First at his second coronation at Winchester, after his return from captivity in Germany. This William resided mostly at his castle of Carisbrooke, and bequeathed three hundred pounds, "a considerable sum in those days," for erecting a monument for his father, and himself in the Abbey Chapel.

Worsley mentions one other Earl who was interred at Quarr, namely Baldwin the Fourth but he was a minor when he succeeded his father and died young. Now it seems to me, taking all these circumstances into consideration, that the remains above referred to are none other than those of Earl Baldwin; the female next to him, Adelina, his Countess; and that on the right hand of his father, William de Vernon, presuming that his body was buried in the same tomb with his parents, and one monument erected for both father and son.

Another author tells us that a few years ago the foundations of the church were uncovered, and the vaults which had been previously rifled and filled up with rubbish, were discovered. We must also take into consideration the feelings which would be naturally associated with the name of the founder of such an institution as this Abbey at the time of its dissolution, and I must confess that I cannot look down with proud contempt upon the name of Monastery and identify it with the worst errors and corruptions, and with reminiscences of nothing but vice and profligacy, because the monastic walls in those days preserved inviolate the Word of God and rescued from oblivion the teachings of Apostolic men. Their roof also afforded a lodging to the weary traveller, and their hospitable board supplied the poor and destitute with food. They also afforded a Christian home for the lonely, and means for the exercise of religious zeal and self-denial.

It must also be remembered that this Abbey was one of the earliest of the

Cistercian Order in this kingdom, and the monks of this Order brought the science of agriculture, more than any others, to a high state of perfection.

"Who with the ploughshare clave the barren moors,
And to green meadows changed the swampy shores?
The thoughtful monks!"

Looking at all these circumstances the name of Earl Baldwin would be as "familiar as household words" in the minds of the recipients of his bounty in those unsettled days of Bluff Harry; and although the means were removed which enabled "the sad and solemn priests to sing for Baldwin's soul," yet some friendly hand might out of respect due to so great a benefactor have preserved his remains and those of his Countess and son from further destruction, and re-interred them in the careful and modest way I have described above.

I am, Sir, your obedient servant,
Edward Harris
80, Union Street, Ryde, January 7th 1857

Editor's note: the whereabouts of these bodies is now a mystery.

ABOUT THE EDITOR

Nick Hammond worked with Margo Williams for the last 18 years of her life, as her personal assistant. Born in south east London, he worked as a Public Relations professional until a visit to the Isle of Wight inspired him to change his career.

"My meeting with Margo truly was a life-changing event. Until that moment I had never thought much about ghosts. I was invited to accompany Margo out on 'digs' as she called them; occasions when ghosts indicated there was something important to them that they had lost or buried, like a keepsake or other treasured possession.

If I was at first sceptical, it wasn't long before I was as amazed as all those other people who joined in her ghostly adventures; for more often than not it was I who found it buried in unturned ground. There was nothing theatrical about what she did, just a warm-hearted down-to-earth openness in helping those who needed it.

I also accompanied her into the homes of people who contacted her, asking for help in removing unwanted paranormal presences. It was the look of pure relief on the householder's face when we returned after; or the many, many letters thanking her for how much she had helped, that I realized what an extraordinary gift this woman had been given; and also the beautiful way in which she used it; for she worked without fuss or expectation of reward, asking only for a donation toward her expenses in getting to them. She did it quietly and professionally.

From then on I stayed with her, and encouraged her to visit some famously haunted sites and buildings, to see what happened. She has helped so many people with her extraordinary gifts, the living and the dead, if that is how we choose to think of them. These books represent my time with Margo, our work together; written together."

CREDITS & SELECTED BIBLIOGRAPHY

Thanks to Lisl, at Dragonfly eBooks for her help with the book.
Visit dragonflyebooks.co.uk

Children of England: the Heirs of King Henry VIII. Alison Weir. Pimlico, 1996.
Ghost & Divining Rod. T.C. Lethbridge. Routledge & Kegan Paul. 1967.
Lancaster & York, The Wars of the Roses. Alison Weir. Arrow, 1995.
London Town Past & Present. W.W. Hutchings. Cassell & Co., 1909.
Nelson's Guide to the Isle of Wight. W.H. Davenport Adams. Nelson, 1865.
Nunwell Symphony. Cecil Aspinall-Oglander. The Hogarth Press, 1945.
"Our Island" In War And Commonwealth. Paul Hooper. Cross Publishing 1998.
PLUTO Pipe-line Under the Ocean : the Definitive Story. Adrian Searle . Shanklin Chine, 1995.
Royal Palaces. Olwen Hedley. Robert Hale. London, 1972.
The Companion Guide to London. David Piper, Harper Collins, 1964.
The Hamlyn Book of Ghosts in Fact & Fiction. Hamlyn, 1978.
The History, Topography and Antiquities of the Isle of Wight. W.H. Davenport Adams. Smith Elder & Co., 1856.
The National & Domestic History of England. W.H.S. Aubrey. James Hagger.
The Oglander Manuscripts, County Records Office, Newport.
The Plantagenet Chronicles. Dr Elizabeth Hallam, George Weidenfeld, 1986.
The Royal Prisoner. Charles I at Carisbrooke. Jack D. Jones. Trustees of Carisbrooke Castle, 1978.
Tower of London. Christopher Hibbert, Reader's Digest. Wonders of Man Series, 1971.
Tower of London, 900 years of English History. Kenneth J Mears, Phaidon Press, 1988.
Windsor Castle, an Illustrated History. Sir Owen Morshead. Phaidon, 1957.
Windsor Castle in the History of the Nation. A.L. Rowse. B.C .A., 1974.
Yarmouth Castle. S.E. Rigold, H.M.S.O., 1958.